~

Tales from the Field:

Lurchers and Terriers

~

by *Penny Taylor*

ISBN 978-0-9567029-2-0

All images, photos etc are copyright of the author, Penny Taylor, unless otherwise stated.

Published by Skycat Publications, a subsidiary of Magdalene Technology.
www.skycatpublications.com

Designed and edited by Ian Kossick, Skycat Publications

Printed by Lavenham Press Ltd, Arbons House, 47 Water Street, Lavenham, Suffolk CO10 9RN
Telephone: +44 (0)1787 247436
Fax: +44 (0)1787 247436

Disclaimer
Many of the tales in this book took place before the current restrictions on hunting with dogs
in the UK, and readers should acquaint themselves with the laws in their respective countries
when using dogs to take game or carry out pest control activities. Where any activity
happened after the ban it was in accordance with the regulations as they stand today. The
author in no way wishes to encourage people to break the law, and any accounts of the illegal
taking of game should be viewed as purely fictional.

Some of the photos in this book are pre-digital and have been scanned into the computer
from prints, hence their lack of quality. Most of these were taken by fellow hunters at the
time, therefore my apologies for not including their names, but time has dulled my memory:
t'was a long time ago! Otherwise, all photos are by the author.

Cover photo by Andy Toyne.

Contents

Me and Whispa, my first lurcher from the rough-coated line created by Anne Powers, circa 1990.

About the Author

Penny lives in Cambridgeshire with her partner Andy, their lurchers, terriers and ferrets. A 'hunter' from early childhood, which was spent on the Cornish moors where anything that wriggled, walked or ran was of interest, Penny has a keen interest in hunting dogs of all types, though the canines which sparked her interest in hunting with lurchers were the Irish Wolfhounds she kept in her youth, one of which managed to catch rabbits on a regular basis.

Though preferring to be labelled a hunter for the pot, targeting edible game, Penny uses her dogs for pest control as well, and though lurchers will always be her foremost love, her terriers play an important part in many of the tales in this book.

However, getting inside the minds of her domestic predators is what Penny finds the most fascinating, together with the almost symbiotic relationship the hunter has with his or her hounds. This book contains detailed accounts of hunts, and shows a deep understanding on the part of the author when it comes to analysing the behaviour of both the hunter and the hunted.

Penny has also written a maintenance book for lurchers and sighthounds (*Running Dog Maintenance*) and is a regular contributor to the *Countryman's Weekly* magazine. Penny is currently working on the manuscript of a Lurcher rearing and training manual.

Also by Penny Taylor

Running Dog Maintenance
published by Skycat Publications 2010

~ Introduction ~

~ ANACHRONISM ~

Definition: *something or someone that is not in its correct historical or chronological time, especially a person that belongs to an earlier time in history.*

~ HUNTER ~

Definition: *a person that hunts wild animals for food or sport. Also, a dog that hunts for food or sport.*

I **am an anachronism. I am a hunter. The two should not be incompatible, but they are seen to be so by the greater majority of other humans from so called 'civilised society' in the 21st century.**

My body has been born into an age of human technological advancement and brilliance, but my spirit is moved by a way of life which was dictated by the primal need to survive off the land we had walked for thousands of years, long before humans laid waste to nature, and our shrinking green places were still habitat for large beasts of prey and predators.

Am I no more than a surviving relic from that bygone era? No. I am also a modern human, blessed with a 21st century brain and emotions, and I certainly would not have to starve if I didn't hunt. How then, do I reconcile that primitive need to hunt, to bring death to wild animals using dogs as my weapons? How then, does my conscience, born of education and a certain morality of upbringing, justify my attitude to killing?

But is there really any need to justify my actions? I have hunted all my life. My father was both hunter and admirer of wildlife. He was also an entomologist, a 'bug man', and he instilled into my very soul a curiosity and passion for all things that wriggle, walk, run or fly. Did I merely inherit, through his genes passed down, those interests? But where did his need to hunt spring from? Robin Page, in his book, *The Hunting Gene*, speaks of our genetic heritage, our need to hunt; the pursuit of game, and its most natural conclusion: the kill.

My father hunted to bring meat to the table, with gun and dog, in the days when we were truly poor, financially speaking. Money might have been short in those far-off days during the early 1950s when we lived on the Cornish moors, but we were rich indeed in so many other ways. As a child, whose every spare moment was spent watching and hunting for the things which flew, crawled and scuttled their way through the small jungles of our land, I never imagined how lasting that legacy would be, and how it would shape my life as an adult.

Nowadays, we have no need to hunt at all. The supermarkets are full of meat. Poverty, true poverty, is a thing of the past, yet still I feel the need to hunt. I don't shoot. I do not trap or snare. Hunting with dogs is my passion. Without them, I wouldn't hunt at all. I've never felt the need to aim a gun at a high flying bird, or sit tucked out of sight in a high seat, waiting for the wary deer to pass below my hiding place. Even the ferrets are merely tools to extricate rabbits from their warrens; warrens which have been marked by a dog, who tell me there are rabbits to ground; my enjoyment comes from watching the dog as it hovers over the warren, poised to snap up the bolting rabbit. I wouldn't go ferreting without a dog.

So my hunting is done through my lurchers and terriers and it is the dog work which excites me; I live the life of the hunter, vicariously, through them. I watch them course and catch their prey. I urge them on silently, my heart beating to a faster rhythm, to that ancient beat, the drumming of life as it washes through my veins; and time stands still as I witness that most ancient of dramas unfold on the field, where stamina and speed combine in one perfect creature, evolved by man over thousands of years.

Even the slower work of the nose dog as it surges back and forth in front of the beating line on the shoot; even that strangely curtailed type of hunting where the dog is merely provider of sport for the guns, where the natural conclusion of such work would be to catch, but is not; even that form of hunting arouses

I watch my dogs home in on that scent.

in me a quickened interest as I watch the dog moving across the field, nose down, hard at work as it unravels the mysteries of scent which leads to warm flesh. The dog lives through a medium which fascinates me. My nose will never be able to tell me where lies the hare or the pheasant, where sits the deer, secretly hidden in briars. And when even my diminished sense of smell can detect where the fox has passed by, I am unable to locate its precise position in cover, but I watch my dogs home in on that scent, and find their quarry. They are truly at one with a world which has been lost to my impoverished senses.

My dogs complete my life, and they offer me the chance to revel in the search and subsequent pursuit and kill. They awaken in me that ancient spirit, that ethos which forces us to fulfil some almost forgotten and basic principle: the principle of life and death in its most direct and pure of forms.

Only the hunter feels life so keenly; an emotion as sharp as an intake of breath on a frosty morning. Only the hunter sees death as a daily event. To truly appreciate life, you must face death, and whilst most hunters nowadays seldom risk their own lives, we risk our dogs' lives each time they hunt. Even a rabbiting dog may risk life when it runs hard across land which spells danger at every step; one wrong foot and life can be over, faster than the seconds it took for the sperm to enter the egg, when life first glowed in the dark sinuous depths of the canine uterus.

To the outsider, the non-hunter, it might seem as though we are obsessed with killing, but there is so much more to those that hunt with dogs and hounds than the race against death; so much more than simply being an observer of dogs dealing death to an animal, a creature we term prey.

There is also a symbiotic relationship between hunting dogs and their humans. There is that conspiratorial glance between dog and human; that recognition between predators. We need their skills to fulfil our dreams. They need our place as protectors and leaders in this modern land where dogs can no longer run free and wild. We've modified their genes to suit our desires, and they give us the old ways once more; life in the shape that our ancestors carved out for themselves: the life of the hunter.

I feel truly sorry for those humans who will never breathe the fresh scent of blood from a kill, who will never experience the pride and the passion we feel for our hunting dogs. This might sound arrogant, vain or downright condescending, but I have seen how the meat on my table has lived and died, and I feel a connection to the forces that created our world, and its inhabitants, in a way that the average supermarket shopper can never appreciate.

My dogs are truly alive. Each time I step into the field, my dogs are alert, their ears, eyes and noses attuned to the potential for prey. They are hunters. I am a hunter, albeit a humbled, useless specimen when compared to their stream-lined, muscled athleticism. I am unable to gallop alongside my four-legged allies. I need them more than they'll ever need me when we're out in the field, and that is why I spend my life with them, relishing our differences, basking in our mutual need to seek out and catch, and in the sameness we both feel as predators.

This book is a collection of tales from my life spent hunting with dogs. Most of the dogs featured were, and are my own. They were, and are today, no more and no less skilled or brilliant than the multitude of working dogs that belong to like-minded hunters the world over. I can only speak for my own dogs; dogs with which I have hunted over the years, dogs which I've bred, reared, trained and loved, and buried at the end of their lives.

I have written about them as a testimony to all hunting dogs of whatever breed or type; as a tribute to their skills and to their exploits, and as a record of their lives and a salute to their collective canine souls. Many working dogs die young, much younger than those pets which seldom leave the safety of the local park or garden. Hunting is dangerous, especially so for the fast dog, be they pure-bred sight hound or lurcher. Few are those which make it to old age unscathed. I believe that they wouldn't have it any other way.

Although I mourn keenly the early demise of such dogs, especially those which should have had years before them, I try to remember that oft quoted proverb: *"In this world, I would rather live two days like a tiger, than two hundred years as a sheep"* (Tipu Sahib, c1750-99, sultan of Mysore, India, to whom this saying is attributed).

I hope you enjoy my 'tigers' tales.

Penny Taylor

5

~ A Hunting Life ~

It is all too easy to remember dogs long gone and to relive their exploits and successes through memories which are slightly biased; all too easy to immortalise their strengths, conveniently omitting to dwell on their less positive traits. But what is perfection? Why do we put so much emphasis on this weird state of being? After all, no thing alive is perfect, no dog, man, woman or child. Why should anything be perfect?

After all, it is only humans who desire things to be perfect. We want everything to be good. We want to be happy, to own the best dog, to live without fear or stress. Centuries of religious teachings have told us that we are fallible, that we are somehow bad, that we need to try and be better, that our lives are a punishment for that 'original sin', that we can't be perfect until we die!

Animals, without their consciousness of self, don't have to worry about being 'perfect' or 'good' … they simply are. If a dog misses a catch it doesn't berate itself with 'could have tried harder', or 'shouldn't have done it like that'. Dogs learn, hopefully, by their mistakes, without beating themselves up if they fail. If only people could live in the same way!

Society tells us that we should strive to be successful in a materialistic world. The message which flows through our every waking moment, via media both visual and auditory, is that wealth brings happiness. Sure, it would be good to have enough money, not to worry about paying the bills, not to have to spend endless hours worrying about how to afford this or that. But does money really bring happiness? Not having any money at all

Opposite: Summer hunting gives young dogs confidence and hones their skills.

brings misery that's for sure, but lots of money doesn't bring true happiness either. Not for me at any rate.

I know one thing for sure … that I'm only truly happy and at ease when watching my dogs working in the field. Maybe I'm a bit weird! But my real satisfaction, the joy, and the deep sense of something fulfilled, is when I'm with my dogs and they've achieved their aim. When hunting with dogs I can lose my frustration with this modern world. I can immerse myself completely in action, in pursuing a way of life that mimics the day-to-day struggle for survival that our ancestors lived for real … every day of their lives.

Is that why we hunters do what we do? Is the need to hunt quite simply a means of escape from a life too bound up with laws and constraints? Of course not. It goes deeper than that, and even after so many years hunting with my dogs, I still get a little glow of satisfaction when even a small meal of rabbit is caught. It's only a snack for a pack, but it represents life. It represents not starving to death. When a bigger meal comes our way, the satisfaction is much greater. To the primitive mind, a large kill keeps starvation at bay for longer than such an insignificant catch. I believe that this is a feeling which our hunter-gatherer ancestors knew very well, though they may not have put it in words as I'm trying to do.

I also believe that a dog's intensified drive for large prey must stem from this ancient instinct, and is a drive to kill something big enough to really refuel those batteries. It is the knowledge that large kills allow the pack to survive, offering the calories necessary to reproduce successfully, and to allow the young to grow strong and swell the numbers of the pack. But killing large prey is more dangerous for the predator, more dangerous than taking a rabbit snatched from the hedgerow. Do dogs perceive the increased size of the prey as an increased threat to their survival? Is their satisfaction in bringing down a large animal commensurate with that danger? Or do dogs simply see a large, warm blood-filled target, a mobile larder full of all those extra calories?

Am I being too imaginative in my suppositions? Probably! But the feeling engendered by a larger kill is very real; at the risk of sounding as though I've imbibed of a chemical mood enhancer, (yeah man) … the vibes are good. The heaving ribs, the slowly waving tails, the lolling tongues and the eyes, squinted with

The Airedale fights her way out of the thorns with a tiny rabbit.

fatigue, are shining with success. All these things speak louder than any words.

~ WORKING TOGETHER ~

In a pack hunt I am, for the most part, more of a spectator, albeit a leader and organiser of sorts. The dogs are the ones doing all the work, but my part is crucial because I, with my bigger brain and my reasoning powers, am scanning the area from a distance, looking for places where the prey might lie up. I am responsible for taking them to the places where we can hunt, but then it's up to the dogs.

Building a cohesive unit takes time. It takes time in the field for each dog to know how the other one operates, especially when you're working with dogs which don't pack naturally. Lurchers and terriers are not like foxhounds or beagles; they've been bred to work solo, though with practice they can form a truly amazing group, just so long as you make sure to weed out the overly independent, those which would rather go-it-alone.

There's no point in pack-hunting if one terrier goes off in a straight line like a train for no reason at all, taking the other dogs with it. Steadiness is one of the most important qualities when selecting dogs which can work as a pack. I've a young terrier at the moment. On her own she's not bad, she has a decent enough nose, and she's mad keen. But she's over-excitable and easily influenced in all the wrong ways. She can't think for herself if there are other dogs in the picture. She only has to spy another dog which is moving at more than a snail's pace and she thinks a chase is on, and she follows, yipping and squeaking like some kid's demented toy. What should have been a steady search for scent becomes a crazy dash after nothing at all; one wrong 'un can ruin a pack in no time if you let it.

Some dogs are special, and I've been very lucky indeed to have had several such 'special' dogs in my life; dogs with whom I've had a bond which goes much deeper than the normal relationship between owner and canine. Why this happens I've no idea, and each of my special dogs have been poles apart in both temperament and type, though they've all been exceptionally intelligent.

Scientists would say it's all down to the genes, a complex chemical arrangement of DNA and good fortune. I don't care what you call it; some dogs are just way up there along the evolutionary scale of the species, understanding far more than most, and able to communicate with us in subtle (and sometimes not so subtle) ways. Such dogs make their needs and desires very obvious to those people who are sufficiently aware and observant. If you work on this mutual awareness you will find that your dog will make as much use of you as you of it, telling you with a piercing look what it needs from its owner.

For example, you are out on your own, just you and one dog, and that dog marks a rabbit in cover. This lurcher is far too smart to go bouncing into the cover in the vague hope that the rabbit will flush in exactly the right place. Instead, the dog stares at you for a moment, before staring just as pointedly into the depths of the bramble.

Really dopy humans may need a few lessons from the dog, a few more intense stares in your direction and back to the bramble before the penny drops! *Ah ha! You say to yourself, I should help flush this rabbit! I know that I'm not fast enough to catch a rabbit when it bolts, so I have to be the terrier.* Now it's your turn to be smart, and you leap into the bramble, trying hard to stay upright and avoid crashing face down in the thorns: this bull-in-a-china-shop approach is sometimes quite effective in putting a rocket under the unwary bunny as it sits tight within its safety-cage of thorns, and it bolts like a bullet, to be snapped up immediately by your trusty ally ... well, that's how it works in theory! Not always in real life, but you get my drift.

I realised early on that small dogs are much better than humans at getting rabbits to bolt, which means that I also get to see all the action from outside the bramble, rather than thrashing around in the depths, getting stuck, tearing jeans and generally wondering why the hell I wasn't born with the legs of a kangaroo.

Teamwork isn't just about the human saying: "Me say, you do" to the dog; it's as much about learning to read your dog's mind and allowing yourself to be guided by these hunters who know more about the where, the why and the how of quarry than we'll ever do ... providing you give them the opportunity to learn.

I feel a kinship with my dogs. We are both predators, human and canine; I think of them as my allies and conspirators in that great and ongoing quest, the perpetual hunt. We live for the hunt; we're on standby until we can get out once more and scour the land in our eternal search. How can a dog be a friend, you might ask? Friendship is a human concept, or is it? My dogs have best friends within the pack, and these are the dogs which gravitate towards one another, who play together, who work and sleep together. Of course dogs have friends, if you let them.

If you keep your dogs solitarily in kennels, they can't form these relationships with each other. They need to live as a family or pack in order to form such friendships. Do these friendships affect the efficiency or success rate of the pack? I have mixed views on this point as I've seen dogs which are not used to working together form a great team when working cover, BUT each dog was already accustomed to working with other dogs and over that type of land. Even humans need time to form a cohesive unit, a group who work as one, rather than a collection of individuals each following their separate paths. Teamwork takes practice.

However, keeping dogs in pack situations makes too many demands on the owner for most people to either want to or be able to live like this. You have to be there, on hand, for much of the time. You have to adjudicate when squabbles arise, and you have to be aware of every nuance of tension or the potential for problems between individuals.

During the golden age of hunting, back in medieval times when hunting was both a sport and a necessity, the wealthy landowners, lords and royalty kept numerous hunting dogs at their castles, and it was usual for a 'dog-boy' to take care of the hounds. The dog-boy would have been but a lowly lad, a scruffy tyke who lived with the dogs in their kennels. His presence in the pack was said to make the dogs more 'human' (*The Sword in the Stone* by T H White and also *Le Livre de Chasse* by Gaston Phebus 15th century) but in reality, this lad would be the one who knew each animal individually. He would know when they were ill, and know if their regime needed changing; he'd know whether or not they co-existed peacefully with their fellows, and he'd know when to keep in season bitches apart from the dogs, unless they were to be used for breeding. The dog-boy would

A delicate retrieve of a sodden rabbit caught after the floods.

have been indispensable to the huntsman who actually worked the hounds, and no doubt, if the dog-boy was made of the right material, he'd move up in the ranks over time, taking his place as part of the overall hunting team.

Nowadays, many working dogs are kept isolated, singly in kennels, apart from other dogs. Neither do they hunt as part of a group in the field. I know that hunting methods have changed over the years, and there is little need nowadays for huge mixed packs of hunting dogs, but for those people who run a bobbery pack, a small bunch of mixed types, it is well to remember that whilst over-familiarity might breed contempt when putting certain types or breeds together in a living situation, the best working pack is made up of dogs which understand the talents and skills of each and every member. And they can only do that by prolonged and regular exposure to game in the field.

I would never consider keeping terriers and lurchers together, either in kennel or house. Terriers are warriors, and even the most amiable and tolerant of terriers have a habit of becoming contemptuous of authority if given the chance to overstep the mark. Size matters! A terrier is well aware that its size and strength are nothing compared to that of a lurcher, and it can put them on edge. You can practically see a well-socialised terrier gritting its teeth in an effort not to respond when challenged by a bigger dog; one that the terrier knows full well can put it away for good if challenged too often or wrongly.

Of course, a terrier which hasn't grown up around big dogs is a different matter. Such a terrier, defending its bed or its bone, will come very unstuck if the big dog decides to teach it a lesson in manners. It's not the terrier's fault. It's us, we humans, who have created the terrier to do battle with sharp-toothed quarry which might be larger and stronger than the dog itself. We can't complain when our small warriors see red when threatened by another dog, because we've made them what they are.

But they work so well together, when there's no silly jousting for position, and when all noses are firmly fixed on the same goal. Do the terriers reason things out like the lurchers? Not in the same way. Terriers are blinkered, focused only on the warm scent of their prey; their minds do not reach out and wrap round a problem to think up an alternative game plan, and only my older veterans have slowed down enough to use their heads to anticipate things like bolts and double backs.

Confidence is of great importance when either hunting with a pack or just one dog. It is vital to build trust between you and your dogs and they need to know that you'll not lie to them when you're looking for game. I hate to see people who urge their dogs on to investigate a particular patch of cover, making the sort of sounds which indicate they've seen some animal when in reality there's nothing there at all. Gee-up your dogs in this way and they'll soon learn that your word counts for nothing; they'll learn to rely on themselves alone, and because you've shown yourself wanting, your control over them will lessen as well.

I love pack hunting; the bustling, busy rustling of the terriers bursting through cover, and I love to see the big dogs following the hunt, placing themselves in the gaps between brambles, anticipating the bolt. I like to see them learning how to do this. Which young dog is intelligent enough to stand still, listening and waiting for something to burst from the dense undergrowth and which young dog is just too daft or too excited to learn much at all in these situations?

I like a dash of pack dog in my terriers: a drop of Beagle blood. Getting the balance right is the tricky thing. I need a pack to work more or less at my feet, to be called quickly to where I want them, and I don't want a dog which just drifts towards the far horizon, nose glued to the floor on an old, and for me, useless scent. I have to read my dog correctly as well. I have to understand when a dog is following a hot, good scent, one that will lead us quickly to prey. And to do that I have to understand each and every individual perfectly ... this too takes time.

My own lurchers know from experience almost straight away what game the cover dogs are working. Of course, the lurchers have noses as well and they often get the air scent of their quarry long before the nose dogs have found and flushed their target, but they also know, from the intensity of baying or yapping, what prey might leap out from the cover.

My terriers have a high-pitched yap when working rabbits. "Yip-yip, yip-yip" they bark, as they push the rabbit back and forth through the runs beneath the brambles; but the baying for fox is harder, more urgent, less frustrated and a damn sight more meaningful. Midge, my now middle-aged, tri-colour mongrelly Russell, is often silent unless she is running right on the tail of a rabbit, only yapping harshly to move a bunny which has hidden itself in a corner she can't quite reach.

Midge is vastly experienced. She has been working cover since she was five months of age, and there isn't much she doesn't know about scent, or the owners of that scent. Even in difficult conditions she knows how to operate, searching the places deep in the shade where lingering scent is stronger. She knows how to lift her head to catch the faintest of air scents, before homing in on the trail on the ground, ears cocked for the slightest noise in the surrounding jungle of brambles and reeds. Very often she'll pause, and listen, crouched motionless in a run beneath the arching mounds of thorns and leaves.

Scent hounds have been bred into various shapes and sizes to optimise their ability to follow a scent. They have longer ears, which drop forward when the hound puts its nose to the ground, and this helps to channel the scent into those sensitive nostrils. Midge has little ears, but she seems to follow a line with no problem at all. We humans can only guess at how a dog sees its world through those convoluted nasal passages. I try to imagine a world which is driven by smells which only a dog can experience: wafting odours criss-crossing the land and the air in a constantly shifting rainbow of exciting, invisible trails. It takes time for the young dog to learn how to read scent correctly, and it's common to see a pup dragging, head down on what we call the tail, or heel line, going the wrong way, running back up the trail away from the quarry instead of following the line in the direction the animal has taken.

Whilst the small dogs work cover, it's up to the lurchers to put themselves in the right place. They need to anticipate where the quarry will bolt, and they constantly assess their places, taking note of where the other dogs are as well. They use all their senses: eyes, ears and noses, altering speed and position, tense and hungry for the chase.

Take Starlight, now old and grey of muzzle, thin-muscled and worn from a life time of hard hunting. She's sitting on the sofa across the room as I write, curled up, though not asleep. Her eyes are slightly open, but unfocused, almost as though she is day dreaming, remembering past exploits. She may be ancient and weak compared to the young dog which used to be the star of many a hunt, but take her out and let her smell muntjac or fox, and her stride springs firm over the ground again, and her great eyes sparkle with the thrill of the hunt. The flesh may indeed have grown weak, but that mighty spirit is still as full of fire and life as it was in her youth. I hope she dies in the field, making one last supreme effort to bring down her quarry, but I know that is unlikely to happen. Life so long maintained; that sense of self preservation so finely in tune with her drive, she won't go out with a bang. And the whimper I dread will be of my making when it comes to the end.

From *The Hollow Men* by T S Elliot. *This is the way the world ends. Not with a bang but a whimper.*

~ Some Hunts from the Memory Bank ~

~ THE ORCHARD HUNT ~

We used to do fox drives, before the ban made foxing with lurchers illegal. One of the best places was right next to a village; a country village, but a village nonetheless, and over the years, gradually repopulated by people who see the countryside as somewhere sweet and Disney-fied, a playground for dear little furry beings who co-exist in honeyed harmony with one another.

The whole area was overrun with foxes, which were drawn in from the fenland marshes by several free-range poultry farms. One of the landowners shot 45 foxes in his back garden over the course of one winter. He actually had an alarm system rigged up whereby a long string stretched from a baited chicken coop in his orchard, right through his window to his favourite armchair.

Most of the foxes were shot from this window, but there were always more to take their place, always more to feel the need to scrounge an easy meal of tasty, flightless bird. I can only imagine what his more urban neighbours thought of him, though I guess they were resigned to the occasional bang as it shattered the easy silence of village life. After all, he'd lived in that house long before the more modern estates crept up around him.

An old orchard was one of the foxes' favourite hide outs, situated about half a mile from the chicken owner's property. Its exact location is as follows: The orchard, an overgrown and abandoned rectangular area of around two acres, lay with one long side right up against a new housing estate. The opposite side was open to a field of young trees, then farmland, wheat or rape being the usual crops. One end of the orchard was no more than a hundred yards from the main road, whilst the other gave on to a small neglected field which lay between the overgrown place and the next, younger orchard.

We organised the drives with a mixture of steady, dog-savvy guns, and a mixed pack of dogs. The plan was always the same: to panic the foxes into bolting to either lurchers or guns. Two of the guns would station themselves at the far end of the orchard, hidden either along the hedgerow, or high up on the mouldering

The team on their way to another drive.

remains of some big round straw bales, whilst we, the beaters, and our dogs would stand with our backs to the road at the near end of the orchard. We didn't worry about the side of the orchard which backed on to the housing estate as the six foot, solid wooden fence which bordered the orchard along that side was strong and relatively new, besides which, we couldn't have done much about a fox which managed to clamber this fence and gain safety in someone's back garden.

It was up to me to patrol the remaining long side of the orchard with my lurchers, the side which led on to open fields. We kept in touch with one another via walkie-talkies or mobile phones. At the signal, the terriers and spaniels were released from the road end, and once inside the human-impenetrable fortress of brambles, they were on their own: free to follow their noses where they led. Over decades, the brambles had grown to fill every space between the gnarled remains of the apple trees. No human could push through the place, though my friend Jake did try one year. Let's just say that when the action had finished, he was still attempting to battle his way out of the jungle, accompanied by curses and the occasional shot at a pigeon, made purely out of frustration at his own predicament!

I don't tend to remember years by dates, but rather by what happened at a particular place, and where the quarry was caught. The year of the Bungalow Fox was the first time we did this orchard. It would have been in February sometime, after the shooting season had finished. The air was cold and dry, if I remember rightly, though bright and clear. We used to get a lot of bright, dry winter days in East Anglia, one of the least rained-upon regions in Britain.

The terriers and two spaniels had been entered at the road end of the orchard, and they quickly disappeared under the looping bramble stems. All was silent for a few moments. I had two lurchers on slips, while Starlight galloped up and down the grass track along the orchard side. Starlight had worked loose like this since her youth and I could trust her to use her super-sharp brain to put herself in the right place at the right time. Her judgement was seldom wrong.

She trotted with her head up, continually sniffing the air, stopping momentarily to listen with her large ears half-cocked. Then a terrier yipped, once, twice, and even my human ears could make out the sound of a rustle, the noise as small dogs pushed faster through the undergrowth. Then a shot rang out from the top end of the orchard and the lurcher flew round the corner and out of my sight. No sign of the terriers.

Starlight came back almost instantly, though I was later to find out that one of the guns had shot a vixen as it crept quietly from the orchard, well ahead of the terriers, blending its way through the rough grass to the foot of the bales where the gun had hidden. Luckily the lurcher hadn't seen the action, and she resumed her patrol down the grass track as the noise from the terriers intensified.

Then a chorus of yapping from inside the orchard, more crashing and rustling, and Starlight tensed suddenly and tore down the track before anchoring her feet in the turf, turning hard to come straight back again, past me, her head turned always towards the trees. She stopped, eyes ablaze, and closed her panting jaws the better to concentrate on the scent which wafted her way. I could hear nothing at all, and the yapping had stopped. The terriers had lost the trail.

Then the lurcher lifted her head again ... and again; turning her nose this way and that, and then sprinted away down the side of the orchard once more; scattered grass blitzed the air, thrown back by her hind feet as powerful muscles drove her forwards. For just a second I thought I'd heard a very slight rustle in front of me within the orchard.

Starlight ran back to the very end of the orchard where the terriers had first entered the jungle, and turning to face the trees, she bounced, leaping high in an attempt to see over the low brambles at the field's edge. Then a flash of red exploded out of the orchard side. The fox had sensed the dog's presence, and whilst attempting to run back down the length of the orchard, must have realised that its intended escape had been cut off. It would chance a run to safety in the open, though not from the exit it had been aiming for.

I shouted, though I don't know if I used words. More likely I shouted: "Here, here, here", though the words would have been uttered in a scream of summons, and most likely came out as a sort of howling blur. I saw the fox running ahead of me down the track, then I saw Starlight, coming like a rocket from the left, leaping the low trailing brambles like a grey brindle tiger, and she was only a few yards behind the fox as it sped between the fir trees bordering the back garden of the bungalow which lay right on the edge of the road.

And then I couldn't see anything!

I ran, having released the other two dogs, and heard one howl of outrage. I knew that voice! And as I pushed between the fir trees and saw the lurchers surrounding the fox, Starlight was on the throat, and her face was bright red in the winter sun. They were only a few feet from a thick hedge which ran to the road at the edge of the garden. I knew what had happened as surely as if I'd witnessed the whole event.

Starlight, in a desperate bid to stop her intended prey from vanishing through that hedge, would have reached out and grabbed the fox's trailing brush; the fox would have spun round in defence and ripped her face, and the size of the rip told me that the dog had jerked her head back fast, then gone in again just as quickly to anchor her prey to the ground with a throat hold which would allow no retaliation.

I dispatched the fox with a blade to the heart, and the lurcher relaxed her grip, whilst watching my move from the corner of her eye. She wasn't normally the sort of dog to continue ragging a carcase for long, though if she'd taken a bite I knew that she'd need to avenge her hurt a little before calming down.

This is what I like about the lurchers I keep, the ones which are brave and committed; those that have been bred from generations of working dogs. They aren't fighting dogs, they are killing dogs; with the right amount of brains and drive, they kill quickly. I've seen dogs which grab hold of a fox anywhere, shaking and battering their quarry, oblivious to the fangs fastened in their own hides. And it's damned hard to get in and dispatch a fox quickly if the dog has not got a good throat hold.

This was a good-sized dog fox, and within moments the terriers arrived on the scene, having followed their noses and ears to the end of the hunt. They flung themselves on the carcase, grounding their energy in a delighted and chaotic ragging session. The lurchers turned away, disinterested in this seemingly pointless fracas, and waited quietly for the next hunt. Switch on, switch off. I like that.

The terriers would take much longer for their raging need to extinguish itself. They'd run themselves into a frenzy as they battled their way through the briars on that tantalisingly warm hot scent, and now they shook and worried the red ragged carcase, crunching and shaking in an ecstasy of release. One by one I scruffed and collared them up; no sense in allowing

Muntjac in a back garden.
Photo: Martin Prior.

them to ride that wave for too long, for the longer a passel of terriers works over a carcase, the more likely they are to fall out with each other.

~ THE MUNTJAC IN THE ORCHARD ~

Of course, this orchard also held muntjac. Most dense cover which is left undisturbed will harbour muntjac in my area. They are at times a bloody nuisance, popping out from the smallest bramble when disturbed by a terrier, leading to all sorts of heart stopping accidents, the kind of incidents which leave me gulping for air as I try to steady my racing heart. These 'accidents' normally happen when I'm just out exercising the dogs, unprepared for the action that follows, and all too often in places where such activities would be, to say the least, likely to arouse shock and horror among the dog-walking, bird-watching population.

The lurchers are always listening to the terriers deep in cover.

People might think that muntjac are easy prey for a dog, and in the open, they are; but on their home ground, deep in cover, it takes a lot of luck and determination to catch one of these 'wood pigs'. That's my name for munties. They are not very deer-like to look at, and they have tusks, or at least, the males have tusks, and little sharp-pointed, backward-facing horns. They are altogether very well-armoured critters, and they know how to use their weaponry to great effect.

They are also capable of blasting through seemingly solid brambles at a speed which defies nature. I'm sure that they must shut their eyes when they do this! Where most animals, including the fox, choose known and well trod paths through brambles, a muntjac under pressure from a dog, will literally dive head first into the thorns, leaving a muntjac-shaped gash in the undergrowth. They are not fast per se, but I defy any lurcher to follow them, jink-for-jink, through thick cover, except on the very rare occasion when a smallish dog is right on the tail of its quarry.

Once, two muntjac exploded almost simultaneously from the orchard. The first went away, storming from the end of the orchard across a newly planted field of apple trees. It had snuck down the orchard, evading the terriers, and came out in the open gaining a massive head start on the lurchers. They had run the wrong way, alerted by the small yipping dogs, and the munty almost gave them the slip, running between the young trees, looping left towards an old railway line. Two lurchers caught it eventually, right in the open, and about 300 yards from a pair of dog walkers. Luckily their focus must have been in the opposite direction to this action, and Andy was able to pick up the muntjac and high-tail it back to our own ground.

The second broke from the long side of the orchard only seconds after the first, and my dogs pulled it down before it had gone 100 yards. "Mine", I shouted fiercely as I caught up with them after a quick sprint across a small field of grass. I didn't want the meat spoiling, and the hindquarters will be ruined when there is more than one dog on a kill.

The skin on a muntjac's shoulders and neck is ridiculously thick, armour-plating for creatures which burst through hawthorn and brambles at warp speed. The skin on the hind end of these deer is still tough, but relatively thin when compared to the leathery hide at the front. And just like a pig, the males can be very aggressive, charging a dog if they're cornered. Their fangs are razor sharp and cut through a dog's skin like a hot knife through butter; they may be small deer, but they're armed and dangerous.

The dogs stood back, and I offered up fervent thanks to the common sense which had led me to do away with the fiery Lakeland terriers I had kept before I had stumbled on the Russelly clan. Those Lakeland types had been great at what they did, but they weren't amenable to pack hunting, and trying to get them off a kill was nigh on impossible.

As it was, my obedient pack had amazed one person present that day for the dogs had stood back on command whilst I dispatched the deer. Of course, this person wasn't to know that the apparently effortless control I had over my dogs was the result of many years training, and an authority which brooked no dissent. Pack hunting can degenerate into a mob-fest of blood and guts unless you have absolute control over your dogs when their blood is up and the adrenalin is coursing through their veins. They are in drive, unstoppable, and on a high that has been generated by a successful kill. You need to take them down fast, put them back into passive acceptance of your authority. It takes time and commitment to work a number of dogs in this way, and there's no room in my pack for those who don't accept my word as law.

~ THE VERY FIRST MUNTJAC ~

Let's go back more years than I care to remember, when I first came to this part of the country. I didn't have much of a pack in those days. I had a mongrel Collie of breeding unknown, rescued off the streets of a city. She had a nose to die for. I also had a small Collie/Greyhound, a wimp of a pup, who grew into a nice little dog, though she'd never be more than a rabbiting companion, as a rule. To look at, these two dogs wouldn't have caused any murmurings, they scarcely resembled lurchers, being small and nondescript ... quite a handy advantage really!

Those two caught our first ever muntjac by the light of the silvery moon in the dead of winter, during a rare week of snowfall.

I'd gone out for a walk at night. The few inches of snow had fallen during the day, and being an eternal romantic, I'd decided to enjoy the peace and quiet of the night, lit only by the cold reflection of the moon on the white, shining ground. I wasn't hunting, but you can't take a working dog into places where game abounds and not expect it to hunt.

They must have disturbed the muntjac as it pottered quietly about in the snow. I've often noticed that wild animals, when unused to snow, seem not to realise that they stand out like beacons against the unfamiliar backdrop of shining white. The two dogs pulled down their prey just inside a fence line, and without a weapon to dispatch the animal, I resorted to something I'd seen on a wildlife film. The film showed a lioness, apparently relaxing on a rock near a water hole. She was lying on her back, paws waving in the air, for all the world like a lazy domestic cat. But she wasn't relaxing at all, and into the picture came a young zebra, inquisitive and innocent. You could see its long ears pricked forward comically as it slowly approached the wriggling lioness, nose stretched forward to investigate this strange creature which flapped its paws above its body, thrashing its tail gently.

The lioness allowed the zebra to get to within a few feet, and then she sprang up, grasping the back of the animal's neck with her huge, clawed front paws, and she engulfed the young muzzle entirely in her massive jaws, cutting off its air supply in a second. All she had to do then was wait for the zebra to succumb to lack of oxygen, an easy task given that the animal was only half grown.

I remembered this film as I wondered how to dispatch that first muntjac, and I grabbed its muzzle in one hand tightly, gripping with my hand over both nostrils and mouth whilst I pinned its body to the ground beneath my knees. Within a minute the beast had gone limp, though I maintained my grip until I could touch the eyeball and get no reflex action. I waited a little longer until I no longer felt the throb of its heartbeat beneath my knee, whilst the two dogs sat watching me intensely. We'd made our first kill, together on a white night in winter, and we were mightily proud of our achievement. I was lucky with that muntjac. It had been a female, but some time afterwards, on a later kill, I gashed the palm of my hand badly on the needle-sharp tips of a male munty's fangs as I endeavoured to do my impression of a lion suffocating its prey!

Most hunters the world over, throughout history and even today, prefer a sharp blade to the heart when dispatching large quarry. I find it strange that some people with guns find a knife distasteful and barbaric. They would sooner remain at a distance, removed from the bloody reality of killing by the swift passage of bullets. They are safe from the smell of hot blood and those last seconds of life before it is extinguished forever. Does their physical absence from that reality shield them from guilt? Do they need to remove themselves from the immediacy and reality of death?

It is easy to go and pick up a dead thing from the ground, something which has expired from the bullets which sped from your gun. It is easy to kill from a distance, never breathing the smell of the animal's fear and panic. It is not so easy to place the blade correctly, and with one swift push, split apart the engine of life, the heart of your prey.

Once a dog has pulled down a large animal, one which would take time for the canine to kill on its own, the blade is as quick as any gun; safer and cleaner in many cases. The boar hunters of Australia and the States dispatch their huge and formidable wild pigs by this method, trusting implicitly in their dogs to maintain a strong hold on the boar's ears, so keeping the lethal tusks from turning and slicing into the flesh of both man and dogs.

~ THE MUNTJAC IN THE LAKE ~

Some of the most exciting hunts have been the most unexpected, and unintentional! They have been true accidents, and their memories have been intensified by the adrenalin rush that comes from pure fear ... the fear of being discovered doing something that the law has decided we have no right to do.

I have learned to steer clear of likely brambles on daily dog exercise, learned to stay upwind of the woods and the cover which hold the 'wood pigs' on what is common land, open to all. The problem is that during the breeding season, the muntjac abandon the safety of their more usual haunts when searching

Muntjac doe and young. Photo: Martin Prior.

for a mate; they are likely to wander abroad both by day and by night. It is during these times that my terriers are likely to find them in the most inappropriate places; right next to a well-trodden footpath, for example. Here's what happened one day many years ago, whilst we were out walking our lurchers on land which was normally devoid of anything larger than a rabbit ...

We'd walked down a path right next to a lake, an old gravel pit now full of water. Along the crumbling cliff edge grew brambles and willows, and on the left side of the path was an old bank, then another well-used path, and another bank on the far side of which was a second lake. The whole area was overgrown with brambles, nettles and thistles, interlaced with black-branched sloe bushes with their deadly long thorns. In the summer, rosebay willow herb stretches its tall pink-purple spikes towards the sky, and cow parsley fills in every space between.

In winter, only the bramble stems and bushes remain above ground, lifted here and there into tunnels created by muntjac, badger and fox. The following account took place in early autumn, when the foliage was still thick and green, and the blackberries hung ripening in great red and black clusters. It was a favourite place for pickers of fruit of all kinds, and the ground was marked with the purplish, seed-filled scat of numerous foxes.

One of the lurchers pricked its ears as a terrier scuttled on its unseen mission down through the brambles on the side of the cliff, and up came a muntjac, so fast as to be only a blur. It came up the cliff face like a rocket, and over the path in a shatter of sound to burst through the cover, and five lurchers threw themselves sideways over the bank in its wake. I followed, in my clumsy human way, bent double as I thrashed through the undergrowth; saw nothing as I reached the path, and then, as I gained the top of the second small bank, I saw the muntjac in the water, heading out across the lake, and just in time, a large merle dog throw itself far out from the bank to land in the water almost on top of its prey.

Sweet was a tank, a Collie Greyhound type, built like the proverbial brick out-house. She'd been born at a local animal shelter, and I'd taken her on as a pup. I often thought that there might have been a bit of Bull in her make-up, for I'd not seen any Collie lurcher so strongly built before. She was also possessed of that typically happy, Bully, human-orientated nature, and there wasn't a nasty thought in her head, but when she hit something muntjac-sized it went down hard, and didn't generally get up again. We jokingly called her the pole-axer! She was also a powerful swimmer who loved water, though even Sweet, with all her enthusiasm and natural affinity with the wet stuff, was no match for a swimming muntjac. These little deer can really swim! Their buoyancy matches that of a plastic duck equipped with an outboard motor, and I have never seen a dog which could come anywhere close to matching their speed whilst swimming.

Muntjac waste no time in getting to water when they are hard-pressed for they must know that no predator can catch them once they've left dry land, and Sweet knew this too, having previously exhausted herself in a futile race across a lake in the past. This time she was lucky, and a superlative effort at long-jump took her close to her prey. She made a huge effort, churning up spray behind her like a speedboat, leaving a foaming swell in her wake, and latched on to the rump of the muntjac before it had gained enough distance to make its getaway.

Within seconds Sweet had secured it by the head, and dragged it back to shore, forced to swim sideways awkwardly, where she was met by me and the rest of the pack. Meanwhile, Andy, who had fallen foul of an old barbed wire fence, and had been battling his way through the undergrowth until then, called quietly, in a stage whisper: "People!" I turned, and saw, to my horror, a group of bright anoraks strolling towards the lake, no more than a hundred yards behind us. Not the usual dog walkers, but a large and obviously organised crowd of ramblers, complete with heavy hiking boots, walking sticks and maps. Why these groups need sticks and hiking boots to wander perfectly flat and easy footpaths I'll never know; I guess its all part of getting themselves into the rambler mode!

No place to hide, so we did the one thing which would appear perfectly normal to your average countryside rambler … we sat down. Backs to the lane, we sat side by side on the damp grass at the edge of the lake; our legs resting across the now defunct muntjac, hidden from sight in front of us. (I was thanking the heavens that these deer are small and not fallow or roe-sized!) We arranged our dogs around us, making them sit or lie down in a group as close to us as possible. Fondly we put our arms round each other and gazed out over the water.

We were, to any unsuspecting onlooker, a couple in love, surrounded by our dear doggies; taking in the beautiful scenery before us: a lake surrounded by willows and reeds. The scene was perfect, the water which only moments ago had boiled and foamed in a life-and-death struggle, lapped gently at our feet. The ramblers passed by not thirty yards behind us, blissfully unaware of what they had missed.

Over the years I've noticed that the non-hunting public seldom see what is actually in front of their eyes. In the same way we might not recognise a person if they appear in a place we don't expect them to be, or if they are wearing clothes which are different to their normal attire, so does the public not register the actions of the hunting dog, or they used not to! Nowadays things are slightly different.

Before the ban on hunting with dogs, along with its attendant media publicity, few people understood what lurchers and hunting entailed. Most were totally unaware of what lurchers got up to in the field, and their minds hadn't been warped and disturbed by images of dogs hunting deer and foxes. But that was before ... now most of the 'countryside loving' public are all too aware thanks to the TV programmes which try to depict all hunting with dogs as something illegal and disgusting.

I've even been targeted whilst ferreting, filmed on a mobile phone by a red-faced and indignant passer-by who was convinced that what we were doing was illegal. His mindset was so warped by media coverage that he'd not even stopped to consider that anyone indulging in an illegal activity would hardly have done so in full view of the general public unless they had been of greatly reduced intelligence. He took some convincing of this fact, and only a patiently repeated PR lecture, one which I've perfected over the years in the face of public condemnation, took the wind from his sails ... eventually! He even managed a stilted 'Good day to you' in parting, no doubt impressed by my diplomatic skills and an ability to sway his warped views with a speech filled with logic and common sense. I jest! No amount of reasoned answers will ever convince the fervent anti that what we are doing is right and natural, and these days I merely hope to defuse their anger as best I can.

The following event took place many years before the public had gained the unfortunate awareness they possess today, and I still find it hard to believe that no one realised what was going on at the time. Read on ...

Opposite: Small but tasty.

~ WHAT THE EYE DOESN'T SEE ~

Whilst I've always been cautious by nature, steering clear of the well-trodden paths beloved of the human sheep which, for the most part, comprise the general population, I was on occasion, forced to walk the dogs quickly across the commons, when all I had time for was a short exercise and toilet walk.

One such walk ended with more drama than I could have ever envisaged. My worst nightmare was realised one day, albeit many years before the hunting ban came into force, when my dogs pulled down a muntjac in broad daylight right in the middle of the common on a Sunday morning in full view of numerous dog walkers, cyclists and bird watchers.

Why a muntjac would choose to lie up in a bramble no larger than a beer barrel right in the middle of dog walker central, I'll never know. Was it a stranger to this area? Or had it been disturbed by an early walker, someone out at the break of day? Whatever its reasons for choosing this small clump of cover, it would soon regret its decision, for a tough and determined Lakeland terrier was about to find its refuge.

Marx was a very strong dog, with a nose and attitude all too familiar with those who work this type of terrier. Generations of workers had produced an animal which would never quit, never back down, and more to the point, never, ever let go of something once he had fixed his teeth in its hide. Like Terminator, he would not stop, ever!

He found the hapless muntjac and it bolted away that fine sunny morning, over a post and rail fence and across the short grass of the common. The terrier's barks alerted the lurchers, who were mooching along with no real hunt in their minds. Over the old railway line they leaped, over the fence, following the harsh sounds of the barks.

Of course, once they'd laid eyes on their quarry the chase was soon over, right slap bang in the middle of a flat and open field, not 200 yards from the main footpath. Muntjac aren't fast on open ground and an average lurcher can overhaul them with ease. As I ran, adrenalin pumping through my veins, heart pounding in fear, awaiting the shrill screech from the muntjac, I glanced around me, looking to see who was where, in terms of human onlookers. I reached the scrum, snapped a command at

Marx was not a team player.

the lurchers to stand clear, and crashed to the ground, sitting astride the fallen muntjac, now held fast at the throat by a grim and silent terrier.

It had barely had time to let out a squeak before the terrier latched on to its windpipe, for which I was more than grateful, but I needed to kill it fast and I had no knife. I covered its muzzle with one hand, whilst with the other I sought to control the terrier, who was shaking and grinding his teeth into his prey as hard as he could. My hand kept slipping from the muntjac's muzzle as I struggled with the other hand to throttle the bloody terrier at the same time.

I was strong then for a woman, after years of physical work had given me biceps some men would have been proud of, but as the minutes wore on I could feel my strength going, slipping away, as the effort of using both hands clenched on two separate animals started to take its toll. And I was trying to be inconspicuous as well. Not easy when you're sitting on a thrashing muntjac and psychotic terrier!

Meanwhile, I continued to cast hasty glances around me: two cyclists about 300 yards away, pedalling slowly across the common, coming closer and closer; and a bird watcher, not sure if it was male or female, and this person was much too close, barely 120 yards from the scene of death. And in the distance a family with a dog, ambling slowly across the turf, the man throwing sticks for the dog, which barked and ran aimlessly in circles.

The muntjac was dead now, but the terrier hung on, and the muscles in my hand on his throat were on fire, my fingers cramped and curled and almost useless. No longer with my attention on the munty, I looked for, and reached a stick on the ground, and forced it sideways between his jaws, and twisted, making him finally release his grip, and quickly I threw him backwards away from the deer, lassoing him with the rope lead, and bringing him hard to my side with a sleight of hand which impressed me, though I say it myself!

Was the bird watcher training her binoculars on me, on my dogs? I dared not look in that direction, no doubt due to some silly notion that if I didn't see her then she couldn't see me either! Like a wild animal, I kept my head down, and looked around for somewhere to stash the carcase.

Using the flimsy cover of a nearby growth of thistles, I dragged the muntjac by one foot, to the nearest ditch, about 30 yards away, and all the while the damned terrier was trying to pull my arm from its socket in his attempt to regain a hold on the deer, though my little entourage of lurchers no doubt did much to hide the shape of the deer in our midst as they walked steadily at my side. I slid the carcase quietly into the ditch, which was no more than a two-foot deep depression in the ground, but a few tall nettles hid its shape once it was laid on the ground, and when no one shouted, hollered or tried to approach me, my breathing gradually slowed.

As nonchalantly as possible, I gathered the lurchers to me, put them on leads and left the scene, not daring to look back. I sauntered casually and apparently aimlessly, like any other Sunday morning dog walker, back to the old railway line and then to my van, but my legs were still trembling inside from all that adrenalin.

I looked at my watch, (yes, we had watches in those days, before the advent of mobile phones) and I realised that some friends, who were coming to pick up a pup that I'd bred, should be at my house by now. I hurried home and burst into the house cursing all terriers and the general public alike, to the astonishment of my guests.

I told Andy exactly where I'd hidden the carcase and he immediately set off on his bike: the common was only a five-minute ride away. We had done this in the past, and nobody would think anything of a man on a bike cycling across the flat fields of the water meadows, besides which, Andy often fished the weirs at the far side of the common and he knew the ground like the back of his hand. Over his shoulder he had slung a large game bag, just big enough for a muntjac still supple, one that hadn't yet stiffened in death. The legs folded easily to hide it from sight and with the head doubled back along the body, the flap closed completely on all but the largest of these mini-deer.

I often wonder exactly what the people on the common that morning had seen, if they'd seen anything at all. So many people wander around without ever looking into the distance, even the near distance, whilst others see only what they expect to see. Did the bird watcher think she was watching a harassed owner trying to separate two dogs which were fighting? Or did she really see what was happening but kept her distance not knowing how to react? Were the two cyclists so deep in conversation with one another that they wouldn't have known if an ostrich had run across the field to their left? Who knows? I've never seen another muntjac in that location in over 20 years ... thankfully; but I still remember that day, and the fear of discovery that came with the drama of battling both dog and muntjac at the same time.

Most people never see muntjac despite their large numbers, and I doubt that anyone would have realised exactly the drama played out in the field right in front of their eyes. I carried a knife from then on. It is quicker than suffocation, though somewhat messier! Andy took only half an hour to retrieve the carcase, which he found undisturbed on the edge of the ditch; by which time I'd calmed down sufficiently to realise that I wasn't on the verge of a heart attack; realised too that the dogs had managed, once again, to fulfil their mission in life without landing us all in jail, though I admit that over the following week I did miss a breath each time I saw a police car in the village! Occasions like this can certainly put a few more grey hairs on your scalp, but if I'm truthful, I'd sooner live life on a precipice rather than down in a soft, gentle valley where there's no peril of falling.

We never wasted a carcase, no matter how awkward it might have been to retrieve it later, though once, having been forced to wait until dusk to fetch a particularly large male, I found it half eaten, the hind legs completely demolished and devoid of all guts and internal organs. Not a single intestine remained. Numerous prints on the ground revealed that both badgers and foxes had glutted themselves on my kill, in the space of only a few hours, between from around four to seven o'clock in the evening. I was not a little miffed by the mess that the thieves had made of the carcase, though I neatly folded the remains and stuffed them into my game bag bearing in mind the moral: waste not, want not.

Favour, the lurcher who prefers to work alone.

~ YOU DON'T ALWAYS NEED TERRIERS ~

Whilst terriers are often invaluable to push game out of cover, a good determined lurcher can sometimes force certain quarry to vacate their hiding places just as efficiently. Here's an account of an evening hunt where everyone, including me, just happened to be in the right place at the right time, something which doesn't always happen ...

It was a quiet February evening, just coming dusk and I'd nipped out quickly to give the lurchers a little exercise after a day of incessant rain. The air was now clear, but heavy with moisture under thick, glowering clouds, and I'd decided that the terriers could stay in their runs for one day. There's nothing worse than tramping around with frustrated tykes on couples, especially when scent is strong and all around them, and I wouldn't have dared let them loose at this time of day when all the wildlife was abroad. I'd learned that lesson on more than one occasion, trotting out for a short walk and finding myself digging by lamplight after dark had long fallen!

Scenting conditions were, however, ideal and even my impoverished human nose was twitching at the strong scent of fox which swirled along the hedge bottom. I was ambling along the side of a sloping grass field and on my left was a very high bank which was covered in scrubby hawthorns and brambles; it was well over the height of a two-storey house. To my right lay a sloping field which rose gently away from the bank: just the sort of place for a fox to call home when it wasn't to ground.

At the end of the bank the hedge broke to the left, down the side of the next field, and it was to this hedge that Favour, the light brindle bitch, followed her nose. I was trudging along without paying much heed to what the lurchers were doing, expecting no more than a few rabbits to run in from the field. Hunni and Sparrow made a couple of futile attempts to catch the speeding bunnies as they raced for home, but Favour was strangely preoccupied at the hedge.

I stood watching the dogs, whilst the young black and brindle lurcher at my side tugged wistfully on the lead. She's still a bit mad-headed when presented with a field full of darting, grey shapes, and I didn't want her to race pointlessly around in the dusk, especially not in this particular spot which is strewn with tangles of old barbed wire fences all broken and sagging; the strands are nigh on invisible being rusted and old. I trust my older dogs to use common sense and experience round this place, but a young dog needs to get to know the whereabouts of dangerous obstacles by day, in full light, before chancing its luck on that wire in the dark.

I'm standing about 70 yards from the hedge where Favour is rootling about, and my position allows me a perfect view of the bank side which gives on to the field. As I watch, I see the pale form of a lurcher tip itself carefully over the wire, and Favour disappears into the thorny hedge, whilst Sparrow and Hunni stand watching her with increased alertness. My mental ears prick up as well, for Favour is not the type of dog to bother herself for a rabbit sat tight in a bramble. She's nearly seven years old, and whilst she's not been my best ever dog, it took me some time to realise that she doesn't like working with terriers at all. However, when working alone, without the scrimmaging terriers or silly quick, jostling youngsters to fray her nerves and ruin her concentration, she is actually a very good hunter, quite partial to finding a fox for herself.

Then my young lurcher stands up on her hind legs, balancing herself bolt upright against the pressure on the lead, ears pricked and eyes straining into the gathering gloom of the evening. I hear nothing. Once again, my human ears just aren't sufficiently acute to hear some faint rustle that has surely alerted the dog. I'm still scanning the hedge and the bank, seeing nothing at all, but the young dog leaps forward, launching herself to the end of the lead, and she's pulling towards the open field to my right.

Following her gaze I can suddenly make out a dark low shape moving fast up the slope of the field, away from the high bank. It's a fox! And it's running up the hill, 60 or 70 yards in the distance.

Do I slip her or not? Will she get there before the fox makes the far side of the hill and safety in the thick hedge bottom? Two questions both pondered and ignored in a milli-second, for my hand is already slipping the rope lead over her head, and she's gone, in a pounding of feet towards the fading dark blur on the smooth grass field.

Opposite: "Then my young lurcher stands up on her hind legs ..."

Even in that twilight grey, where all colour has vanished to monochrome hues, where objects become fuzzy and indistinct, I see her turn the fox once, and now they're coming back down the hill towards me. She turns it again, once more, and this time she stays tighter to its tail and she's lunging hard, but then comes Hunni, a pale blur in the twilight, racing towards the two dark shapes which appear almost as one, and before I can see if the youngster has made the strike on her own, the blonde bitch is there and all the shapes stop running at once.

By the time I walk over to them, Favour has come back through the hedge, her rough coat full of thorns and bits of twigs and leaves, I have joined the dogs and the fox is dead. Not a large one, and it appears to be a barren vixen. Whilst I do try to leave the foxes alone at this time of year, the unexpected does happen from time to time, so I was doubly pleased to see that there was no tell-tale bulge in this vixen's abdomen.

I let the young dog enjoy a moment on the throat of her quarry, before calling her off, which she does, albeit reluctantly, before disposing of the carcase discreetly, pushing it down a deep crevice in the side of the hawthorn bank. I pull some dead branches over the spot, and by the time I have finished there is no evidence at all to the casual eye. I never leave a carcase in full view, even if the chances of a passer-by are remote. Less than five minutes have passed since Favour slid quietly over the wire and into the brambles.

I'm pleased with Favour for locating and flushing the fox, but even more pleased that the young bitch has made her first contact with a running vulpine. She's seen several in cover with the terriers, but this was her first meeting with one on open ground, and although she didn't take it single-handedly, it was nonetheless a good introduction to the swift jinks and turns that a fox on the run can offer a dog.

The successful outcome of this hunt just shows how useful it is to keep one dog on a slip, for the young lurcher would no doubt have been charging through the brambles in the wake of the older lurcher had she been loose. She would have missed the opportunity to run that fox in the open. As it is, she's learned a bit more of her quarry's abilities and soon she'll be ready to go out on the lamp after something a bit more challenging than a rabbit.

~ THE SWISS CHEESE BANK ~

We'd been asked to go up to some fen land near the Wash, where the land is as flat as a desert plain, and the sky seems so high and far away that the light from the sun sweeps clear from one side of the world to the other. Sea birds call far in the distance, and the air is filled with that seaweed tang of ozone and saltwater combined.

We weren't expecting to find many foxes, because a dour-faced keeper, who didn't appear too happy to see us on his preserve, told us he'd shot several quite recently. The story of my life! Our host, one of the guns on the shoot who'd arranged the day, seemed unperturbed and I guess it was just a day out for him, result or not. If we did find a fox then the keeper would be even more disgusted with our presence, for that meant he'd have failed in his task ... his attitude made me really, really want to find a fox!

I was in fox mode, determined to find even one. I hadn't travelled for some considerable distance to come home empty handed. We even managed to put up a trio of roe from a reed bed, and only just grabbed the lurchers in time, knowing well that the binoculars of various bird watchers had swivelled to follow our every move from their vantage point on the sea wall bank. Curses!

Having walked the dykes for what seemed like hours, only one place was left to try; a high bank, probably a good 40 feet high, and several hundred yards in length. This bank had been created when machines had carved out a flight pond many years previously, time enough for trees to have been planted and grown to what passed for maturity. They weren't very tall as the bitter east winds from the sea had constantly blasted the seedlings, stunting their growth. There's a saying on the fens that the East wind is a lazy wind; lazy because it goes straight through you! Even with layers of appropriate clothing you can sense the cutting bite of those winds in winter.

The bank was grassed over, and as we approached the mini hill, we could see that whilst foxes may have been culled to the limit, no one had done much about what was obviously a serious rabbit problem. The bank was a Swiss cheese, seeming in places to be more hole than earth, along its entire length; one massive warren or more likely a multitude of smaller warrens, though many would be linked by tiny tubes. I let Sonic run loose. Sonic was the daughter of my original Midge, a line of mongrelised Russells with dashes of Pit Bull and Beagle sprinkled into the mix over the years. Midge came from a family of dogs which had been bred by a virtual recluse of the fens, a chap who kept himself to himself, and bred the dogs because he liked them, which was as good a reason as any. I shall be forever grateful to my then pest control job which had allowed me to happen upon the little pack as I did my farm rounds on the fens, for I'd literally come to a stop in the small fen road when the dogs appeared.

Midge was 12 weeks of age when I met her, and she'd run up to my van as I opened the door, and had jumped in and sat on my knee, squinting at me through her sparkly, triangular-shaped eyes. I did something I've never done before, or since, and asked if I could buy her. After several cups of coffee, taken in the company of Bill, surrounded by generations of his dogs, I went home with Midge, who became one of the best terriers I've had.

Midge's nose had been phenomenal, and Sonic's was better. She'd grown up pack hunting with the rest of my dogs, and learned very early on in her life that rabbits were hunted on top, and that she only went to ground on fox. I knew that I could rely on her not to go to ground on a rabbit, and who knows, a fox might have found the place to its liking, and especially on land where the keeper had patrolled the most obviously used places where a fox might like to hide.

Sonic disappeared as we walked along the top of the bank, vanishing suddenly, and I hadn't a clue where she'd gone. That's the problem with days out in company; you chat and forget to pay attention to the dogs! She had obviously gone to ground, but where? We swept the area we'd just covered, moving back and forth with the locators, but the box was silent. Not a beep, not even a stuttering whine from the thing.

Starlight was looking too, unbeknownst to me, and it wasn't until I heard her whining that I paid her any attention. She had moved ahead some 20 yards, pawing at a hole several feet from the top of the bank. The hole was just one of hundreds, and this one looked no different to all the rest, but the lurcher knew something we didn't. As I slithered down the steep incline, sliding between the small trees, she whined again, and looked pointedly at the hole, then back at me. *Sonic's in there.* She might as well have spoken out loud so clear was her message. My heart sank.

You know that awful feeling you get when you wonder if your terrier has come unstuck from its true mission in life, and gone to ground on a rabbit. That feeling came right to me then, sitting in my gut like a lump of lead, forcing the question into my mind: had Sonic really gone on a rabbit? Surely that hole was too small for even the tiniest fox to squeeze into!

How sad it is to doubt a solid dog. How sad that the human brain, using logic and intellect, ignores the urgent communication from a dog I trusted implicitly! How stupid was I! I quickly got hold of the other two terriers and coupled them up, tying them to a tree at the top of the bank.

Of course Starlight was right; her nose told her where the terrier was, and that there was a fox in the equation. Starlight never marked rabbits in that way; she was of the same mind as

The brace from the swiss cheese bank.

43

the terriers. Rabbits were hunted on top, and foxes were marked to ground. Starlight had often been ferreting, but she never made a sound on rabbits. Only foxes created such desire that a whine of frustration and anticipation was forced from her throat.

We moved up the bank, and quickly located the terrier, less than three feet below the surface, right at the very top of the mound. I could even hear the sound of her claws as she dug on. We broke through, and there was Sonic, stuck fast, though trying to dig on, and even then, my human doubts crept in. Sonic was so small and narrow, she'd never had to dig on before: was it really a fox?

Andy opened up the tube around and in front of her, she pushed on again, and once again started digging, and so it went on, round in a curve, open up, clear the loose soil out, dog disappearing forward once more. Eventually she stopped digging and started lugging, and the rest of the sandy earth was scraped out to reveal the brush of a fox, wedged tight in the stop end.

It turned out to be an average sized fox as well, not particularly small, and a dog fox at that. Oh ye of little faith Taylor!

Soon afterwards Sonic did it again, or was it Midge, her dam? I had three generations of terriers there that day, Midge, Sonic, and Sonic's daughter Silver. If I remember rightly both Midge and Silver were loose at the time, though Silver was yet little more than a pup and I had allowed her to run free most of the day to gain more experience on foreign ground. I think that Midge, the veteran, had found to ground the second time, in a sprawling place of many holes which led to several levels of tubes. Luckily none were deep into the bank, and it had been more of a case of listening to where the sounds came from than digging deep caverns into the side of the bank.

We had a brace from this place and the dog fox bolted down the side of the bank unexpectedly, slipping through the trees, down towards our vehicles, parked on the road way below. One of our party lifted his gun, but realised just in time that he'd have wounded his 4x4 if he'd taken the shot in that direction! No matter, Starlight and the other lurcher were hot on its tail, and snatched the fox from between the parked cars as it attempted its escape.

And the vixen? I can't even remember if it bolted or was taken below ground for I didn't actually see what happened, as I was down on the road, sorting out dogs and fox at the time. Without the lurchers we'd have lost fox number two, once again proving that dogs really are more use than a gun in many situations.

As we sat at home on the sofa that night, Starlight and I, we looked into each other's eyes, reliving the day's events. Starlight has a special look which she gives me after we've had a good day; a sideways, lingering look that glows with the satisfaction that only a dog who loves its life can give. I've only had three dogs that looked into my eyes like that after a successful day or night. The look is intense, prolonged, and whilst most of my dogs hold my eyes like this when they want something from me, only a few are sharing something else, an unspoken link of pleasure at a job well done, a happiness welling from deep inside.

I've been hunting in one form or another all of my life, starting off with insects and reptiles as a very young child. I've also been an explorer of sorts, in my own country. I love nothing more than to venture on to new ground, to search places I've not been in before in that ongoing quest for adventure and ever more game. Is this what makes me a hunter? I can see the way that my dogs behave on new land: they are definitely more excited, keener, looking for the promise of new quarry and kills. It's all very well to trudge round the same land day in and day out, knowing that you may get a rabbit here and there, or occasionally something even tastier.

But to go out for the first time on land which is foreign to me and my dogs is what I love best; we don't know what is around the next corner, and to round a turn in a hedge, or to discover a new place where game might lie up: that is what keeps me going. Each new day, each new place can be an adventure. The adrenalin rush which this brings makes life worthwhile.

INTERLUDE with a Muntjac

HUNTING isn't always about killing, and I know that most hunters will agree with me when I say that sometimes just seeing a secretive and shy creature can be every bit as amazing an experience as the actual hunting of that animal. I think I've had just as many thrilling moments watching wildlife as I have being the instrument of their demise. This photo was a very lucky shot which was taken on a hot June day, mid-morning. I was walking a young lurcher down to the river for a spot of retrieve training, and of course I had the camera with me.

Out alone, just me and one dog, I try to walk quietly, making sure not to tread on twigs or stones which might alert animals to my presence. Young lurcher was on the lead as I came off the bank and on to a green grassy lane which was bordered by trees and thick cover. The sunlight burned through the branches, diffuse and strangely muted by the dense canopy of green; it was almost as if I was in an underwater tunnel of flickering colour, and the air held a heavy, thick scent of lushness and growth.

The old lady was walking quietly towards me, with a half-grown youngster behind her. I could see from her general shape and her ears, as well as the wear to her head, that she was not a young doe; all these things I took in at a glance when I first poked my head round the trees on the edge of the lane. She was wary, though certainly not worried, and even though a slight breeze was blowing from me to her, she didn't appear to have winded us at all.

Closer and closer they came, and as I crouched back behind a clump of weeds on the edge of the path I was at once annoyed with myself for having a dog in tow and thankful that he had his back to the deer, for he'd just seen a squirrel scuttle skywards up one of the huge oak trees that bordered the path. His attention was firmly on the tree, and I have to thank that squirrel for being there, for I'd never have got the shot if my young dog had seen those munties pacing daintily towards him!

Closer, still closer they came; then suddenly stopped. The doe was only about four metres away from me. Her large ears flared like trumpets, and her nostrils quivered. She had smelled something strange in her world. She raised one forefoot tentatively, and in that moment, holding the camera in one hand whilst trying to keep young lurcher completely still with the other, I focused and clicked, the dog spun round, the deer stamped her foot hard, and her young one dived sideways into the brambles.

The doe leaped, turning on her own length, and banging both hind feet on the hard packed earth beneath the grass, set off, not at a gallop, but at a deliberately slower pace, holding the white underside of her tail high to attract our attention. She ran the whole length of the path in plain sight in an attempt to distract the predators' view from where her offspring had disappeared into the dense, green undergrowth.

Young lurcher was doing his impression of a canine kite, yodelling in excitement as he watched the brave doe 'lead' him away from her young one. I held on to him firmly, but of course his antics precluded any more shots. Image stabiliser may be a wonderful invention but cannot cope with the sort of movement generated by a howling, leaping hound! I fully expected the photo to be blurred and shaky, for the lens is quite long and heavy: not suited to one-handed operation at all.

It didn't turn out too badly at all really, and I now have this tranquil reminder of that hot June morning when the wildlife came to me along a leafy green tunnel full of light. Of course, without young dog there to complicate matters, I could maybe have managed to get both deer in the picture, but then again, whenever I take myself and the camera out alone, I seldom see anything much at all! C'est la vie!

~ Elka ~

Elka was the pup that nobody wanted. From an early age she was slightly different to her siblings. When they rolled, fought and played together in a mass of fur, legs and tiny teeth, she sat apart, a glowering black presence in the farthest corner of the box. She seemed withdrawn, not wanting to take her place amidst her brothers and sisters, fending off playful overtures with a snap and a baleful glare which said: *Leave me alone!*

This was a badly-timed litter, born in late autumn, and necessarily confined to a warm, heated shed for much of the winter; as the pups grew bigger, their legs stronger, they needed to enlarge their small world, and spent much of their waking hours attempting escape from their den, desperate to explore a rapidly expanding world as their senses developed.

When they were five weeks old I simply had to allow them access to the cold and wintery garden, unable to stand their cries of frustration and their constant yapping any longer. They needed space, and lots of it. Despite my misgivings, the pups paid no attention to the crystalline grass beneath their feet or the icy concrete of the path, and they raced like tiny furry whirlwinds, back and forth, in an unsteady pack, legs still unused to running. All except Elka, who plodded steadily around the perimeters of her available world. She scoured the garden from top to bottom, occasionally fending off an attack from a sibling, turning and snarling ferociously as a pup slammed into her in high-spirited play.

Opposite: Night falls over Elka's pit.

It started to rain. Freezing drops fell from a dull black sky, and I called the pups back to their shed. They came, panting and shoving, climbing over and under each other, all eager and bumbling, smelling the meat I carried in a large flat dish. All except Elka. She would usually sit unmoving, waiting for the scrum to subside before coming forward to eat her fill: even then, at five or six weeks of age, she didn't like being jostled by others. She didn't have a name then, she was just "Puppy", like the others, and when I called "Puppies!" in a high-pitched voice they'd come running to me.

I counted the pups into the shed, and found one missing. Back into the drenched and freezing garden I went, peering closely into shadowed places where a pup might be cowering and hiding from the miserable downpour. But I found Elka, mysteriously involved in a game of her own, down between the greenhouse and the fence. At first I thought she'd got stuck, but as I reached into the narrow space and got hold of her back end, the front end shook with a rage quite out of proportion to the softness we expect from a small puppy.

I pulled the pup out of the space, her body rigid with fury at my interference, and between her clenched jaws was the tiny carcase of a long-dead mouse. I prised her mouth open gently and as the carcase fell to the ground, Elka immediately relaxed, all trace of possession and violence quite gone. I cuddled the damp pup in my arms, and dried her off with large handfuls of straw once we were back in the shed. She sat on my knee, stretching to lick my face, something she'd never done before. She had until then been one of those pups which turn their heads away when I tried to cuddle her close, but now she seemed suddenly happier, as though something had changed in her head.

The pup became more responsive each day, though you could see that she lived for the 'hunt'. Her nose hit the ground as soon as she got into the garden and she stalked sparrows and blackbirds, leaping into the air as they flew low overhead. People came for the pups, and one by one they went off to their new homes, but no one looked at Elka, who never came out to greet people. She didn't seem scared or worried by the arrival of strangers; she was just anti-social, and the choice was made for me: she was staying. I hadn't decided which pup I was

Seeker, Elka's dam.

keeping as they all had something about them, that indefinable quality I like so much in the lurcher-to-lurcher bred animal. Their dam was Seeker, a three-quarter Greyhound, one-quarter Bearded Collie, and she'd proved her worth as a worker many times over.

The sire was the relatively untried brother of my original stud choice. For reasons unknown to us humans, Seeker had decided she wanted no part of my original choice of dog, a handsome beast who had already proved himself in the field on many an occasion. She had snapped and turned on him viciously each time he laid a tentative paw across her shoulders, the first overtures of a suitor when presented with an in-season bitch.

We tried for two long days to achieve the mating, and finally threw in the towel, calling in on the dog's brother on the way home, more out of desperation than anything. Widget might not have done much work in the field, but he carried the bloodlines

I wanted, the generations of lurcher-to-lurcher blood which produced the decent, multi-tasking animals I liked so much.

Widget was more finely built than his brother, and rougher of coat; a coat I later realised would throw rough-coated puppies, no matter what bitch he mated. The coat length was of little importance to me, and whilst I like the traditional hairy look of a lurcher, it's not the coat that makes the dog. Seeker had taken one look at Widget and turned her tail in invitation; the matter was out of my hands, and with no more than a cursory introduction, he'd jumped on the now-willing bitch and they'd tied.

The resulting pups were nearly all blue or brindle, like their parents, though two were coal black. Elka was one of the black pups, and she was so long in the back that people, on seeing the litter, joked that a Dachshund had got into Seeker's kennel and somehow managed to mate the bitch!

Long of body, short of temper, and definitely not inclined to fuss and grovel around humans, Elka stayed. Whilst the other pups tried their best to be first in the queue for affection from human hands, she sat in the corner, not scared, not worried, just staying quietly out of the way. As the other pups vanished from her world, Elka found herself permanently alone in the shed, and one day she simply followed her dam up the path into the house, chose a quiet corner in the kitchen, and went to sleep with a deep sigh of contentment.

Strangely, I can't remember a whole lot about her upbringing. I was working full-time as a pest controller, often with Seeker at my side. Mundane jobs on the whole: setting and checking mole traps, tramping interminable factory floors replenishing boxes of mouse and rat bait, I scooted up ladders in grain stores, determinedly ignoring that fear-of-falling feeling; that sensation which brings a tingling in the soles of your feet, as you sit on narrow catwalks made from sagging planks strung high above the grain silos. Seeker stayed in the van when I risked life and limb like this, for I'm damn sure she'd have tried to climb the ladders with me.

Elka grew up with very little in the way of formal training. She always came when she was called, she loved retrieving old socks and balls, and from the age of around ten weeks, she came out on our daily mooches each evening after I had finished work. There seemed nothing odd about her at all any more and she fitted in with the rest of the pack with no problem. She never made waves, and despite the lack of one-to-one attention and training, was obedient and willing to please me, though she was never pushy or demanding in any way, unlike some pups which seem determined to annoy everything and everyone in their world. Those are the 'look at me' pups; the ones which continually wind you up with their forceful natures and a desire to test their surroundings to the limit.

Elka was none of those things, and I can't even remember her playing much at all with the other dogs, apart from her mother of course. Seeker's Collie blood had given her the 'playful gene', the genetic inheritance which bubbles over in Collies of all types. The desire to have fun if there's no serious hunting on offer, and she made sure that the pup got plenty of her attention when there was nothing more exciting to do.

Elka grew up watching her dam catch rabbits. Seeker was both hunter and catcher, finder and killer of all things furred and feathered. She was one of only two dogs I have ever owned on whom I can truly bestow the title of all-rounder. Which isn't to say that Seeker was the very best at all the jobs she undertook as she didn't have the gears to take hares on a regular basis given fair law, especially when those hares were at their fittest after Christmas.

I've always taken pups out mooching on the type of land they'll encounter as adults. Elka learned very young that barbed wire was different to the thorns which laced the brambles. She learned to avoid the tines on the carelessly laced wires, whereas she'd push past a bramble with no hesitation. As a winter-born pup, she was just the right age to enjoy the water as spring turned into summer, and she soon showed that she was almost as at home in the lakes as she was on dry land, just like her dam.

I can remember her first rabbit as clearly as if it were yesterday. We were out on our daily ramble around the old gravel pits, and Elka was now around five or six months of age, strong and well-grown. She was tearing through the reed beds with Seeker and two other lurchers and Seeker had put the rabbit out of some reeds at the edge of the dried-up lake bed, as I called it. This was an old gravel pit, now plush with willows, buddleia and reeds all along the rim of the pit. A small 'cliff', just over a metre in height, dropped down to the gravel floor of the shallow pit, and all at once I saw the pup swoop from this cliff down into the reeds.

As fast as she'd disappeared she came back into view, a half grown rabbit in her jaws, and she ran as fast as her legs would move, straight to me, hotly pursued by the other lurchers. Even at such a young age she was almost as fast as the adults, her long body stretching with huge strides across the uneven ground. Elka literally threw the rabbit at me as she came past, going too fast to slam on the anchors. *"Here! Take it!"* and I did, reaching down to grab the stunned bunny before the rest of the dogs converged on our prize. And the pup glanced up at me with a look which told me that I was worthy of her rabbit, that if she had to give it up to anyone, it had to be me. Never let the other dogs get hold of it, it was her rabbit but I wasn't a dog so there was no competition. I was the honorary leader, but more than that, I was THE safe place to be, the place where all things were right and good, the food source, the healer of wounds, and the order which prevailed over the entire pack.

Elka and pups.

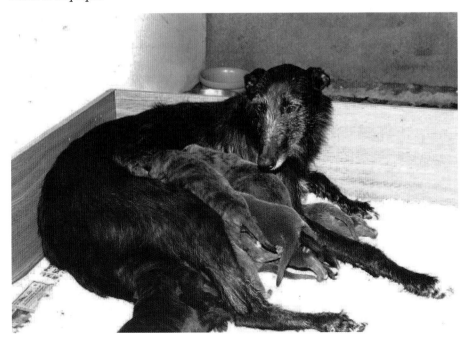

And that was how she behaved for the rest of her life, retrieving her rabbits at a gallop. Rabbits were often caught in a kamikaze strike which ended with Elka upside down in a bramble or bed of nettles. Until she was six years old she caught over 90% of ALL the rabbits we caught by day out mooching. Her strike was phenomenal, her speed awe-inspiring, and her dedication to the catch unwavering. At the time I had Elka I didn't know about things like 'prey drive'; I didn't analyse the whys and the wherefores of dogs; I just took them out and worked them. To me she was just a bloody good dog!

But Elka didn't hunt for rabbits; that was Seeker's job. It was Seeker who worked tirelessly to find the prey, hidden deep in the reed beds or long-thistled fields of set-aside, whilst the catch dog, the goal keeper, her daughter, shadowed the hunter. Being catch dog was Elka's self-appointed role in life. I didn't train her to behave like this, but if you work dogs in number, as a pack, it is normal for each individual to adopt a certain role, to fill in the spaces, if you like, where each dog forms part of the whole jigsaw puzzle that makes a successful pack.

Some people say that domestic dogs are not pack animals, that man's intervention, his artificial breeding of dogs for the hunt, has taken this pack instinct from them. I'd argue the case. Our domestic predators may well be the product of thousands of years breeding, but the ability to hunt as part of a team has never been lost, providing you allow your dogs to form themselves into a unit, a task force, as nature intended.

If you try to force the nose dog, the animal which instinctively wants to range out further afield, to stay by your side, whilst you encourage a different hound to do that job, you'll fail miserably. Just like us humans, each dog is different. Each dog has different talents, and some, no matter what the breed or type, prefer to hunt, keep moving, active and focused on scent.

Dogs will learn that there's no point in the whole pack moving out from the hedge, especially once they have realised that rabbits always run back to cover. Time and again I've seen my dogs look at each other as we enter a field. It is second nature, instinct, for them to assess the strengths and weaknesses of the pack at a glance. They know which dogs are the nose dogs, the far ranging hunters, and many's the time I've seen two dogs move out into a field, only for one to fall back to guard the hedge, realising that this avenue of escape hadn't been covered.

Take that 'goal-keeping' dog out on another day, with different canine hunting partners, and the goalie dog might well become the hunter on that occasion; it all depends on the company out in the field on a given day.

Taking them out together, just the two of them, Elka and Seeker, was a treat for my eyes. They worked in perfect harmony. Seeker was always the hunter, out in the fields of set-aside, nose down, searching, and she'd got the name Seeker because even as a young pup she showed this aptitude. Whilst Elka stayed near the cover, the hedges and warrens, eyes constantly scanning the ground ahead of her dam, watching and waiting for movement, Seeker worked up on the fields. Elka never hunted with her nose, ever, until after her dam had died, and then she just switched jobs, overnight, and started hunting-up as though she'd been doing it all her life.

Elka's mouth was so soft that despite that faster-than-the-eye strike, her rabbits were seldom bruised, and all were delivered alive to hand with barely a hair out of place. I've always wondered how a lurcher, equipped with all those teeth, those powerful jaws, in the heat of the moment, that strike, delivered at a gallop, can pick up a small running prey without harming it at all.

To begin with she threw her catches down on the ground, often too far from me, and the rabbit would jump to its feet and run again, and she'd have to catch it all over again. The pup was so submissive to me, deferred to my authority so completely, that she must have felt unable to hold on to her catch in my presence. Or was it that at all? Did she just hurl the rabbits in my general direction as she came past because she assumed that I would be able to pick them up like a lurcher; that I was just as capable as she was to run down and swoop into the rabbit, as she did?

I guess, with hindsight, that I could have taught the dog to 'hold', but I was young and eager, and more importantly, ignorant of more advanced dog training. Holding was for gun dogs, and to be honest, did I really care if the dog laid the rabbit on the ground rather than delivering it into my hands?

Things changed when we went out on the lamp for the first time. Now we were one-to-one, no other dogs around, no competition for the prize. Having had plenty of day-time practice at catching rabbits, Elka soon cottoned on to the notion of watching the beam of light as it drifted around the inky blackness of a field at night. Her eyes, those glowing amber orbs so like those of the eagle owl, fixed on the shaft of light, and there, at the end of the light sat a rabbit. I could feel her body trembling against my leg, and her hammering heart bounding within her rib cage. This was new!

Elka became good on the lamp quite quickly, though she did have to learn not to over-shoot on the turn. She was unused to picking up rabbits on open ground when they were running for home, and these were very different to rabbits bolted from brambles, but the retrieve thing sorted itself out quickly once she started working on the lamp.

As Elka came back with a rabbit, alive and unharmed, placing it carefully on the ground, the damn thing got up and ran down a hole not two feet away. She never put a rabbit down on the ground again in her entire life. She would come to me just as fast as before, but now she'd stand before me, waiting until she felt that I had a firm grip on the rabbit's hind legs before relinquishing her grip. Problem sorted!

Elka, the dog with eagle owl eyes.

I've been writing about Elka's prowess as a rabbit dog up until now, but foxes were her true calling. Like her dam, who had decided that rabbits were pretty small fry compared to the challenge of that larger, more predatory quarry, Elka met her first fox at the tender age of around ten months. Seeker had taken her first fox at a similar age, and she'd come to me, dragging the carcase back through the reeds with an unshakeable grip on its throat. I'd heard her stumbling through the clattering stems on a winter's day where the shards of ice made tinkling sounds as they snapped and fell to the frozen water of the lake, dragging the carcase as a lion drags a zebra along the ground, between straddled front legs, held wide to accommodate the awkward burden. So did Seeker present me with her first fox, after a hunt I hadn't even known was taking place.

~ HER FIRST FOXES ~

Elka's first was taken in the company of her uncle Merlin who'd come to stay with me for a few days. Merlin made short work of foxes, though he'd learned his trade alongside Seeker, running alongside the more experienced bitch for the whole of his first season. His breeding was lurcher-to-lurcher for many generations, the exact breeds lost in the mists of time, and whilst the line wasn't bred specifically for fox work, most took all quarry, and this dog had made good, growing in confidence and strength until he missed very few of those sharp-toothed pests.

We were walking a wood: a wood on a slight rise of land where slim trees were interspersed with brambles. This was a haven for foxes in an area which flooded on a regular basis. Seldom did we find anything much to ground in this place, as the water table was usually too high to make for a comfortable refuge beneath the soil. The foxes laid up in the brambles and reed beds, out of sight, and as far as the general public were concerned, non-existent. Merlin had disappeared ahead of me, flitting silently between the trees. He was probably shadowing Seeker as she followed her nose along a fresh scent laid only the night before.

As I write today, now under the yoke of that ridiculous law which has made criminals of hunters with dogs, I find it hard to remember just how much freedom we enjoyed back then.

Then, I had no fear as my lurchers hunted up freely, out of sight. Back then, over 20 years ago, there were few ramblers, few bird watchers, hardly any pet-dog walkers, and best of all, no pompous and hypocritical ban which said that it was forbidden to hunt as our forefathers hunted, with dogs and hounds. Seriously, what other law in a supposedly democratic society has, overnight, made criminals of previously law-abiding citizens? Did those suits in their air-conditioned offices ever stop to think just how absurd their law might appear to future generations? Only fascist dictators behave in this way. Enough! I must not get started on the ban (which I refuse to decorate with a capital B!) or this book would be about rules, laws and the stupidity of governments.

Let's get back to Elka's first fox ... I heard a rustle, the scuffle of galloping feet on the soft leafy floor of the wood, then the unmistakable screech of a fox, then silence. I ran towards the faint echoes of that screech, and found Merlin dispatching a large dog fox, and right beside him, his niece. I was just in time to catch her watching her uncle: he was a rib dog, his manner of dispatch was efficient and fast: he'd flip a fox on the run, and in a movement too quick for human eyes to properly register, fasten his powerful jaws round its ribs, exerting such pressure that both heart and lungs were crushed in seconds.

Elka saw him do this, and immediately fastened her jaws next to his, and both dogs crunched on ribs in unison. "Good dogs", I said, and two tails wagged furiously. Once Merlin was sure that the fox wasn't going to get up and run off (do dogs feel the fading heartbeat of their kill as it finally ceases, the last breaths drawn then nothing more?) he was always happy to come away from the carcase. Elka would be the same as she became more experienced, but this was her first taste of what would become her preferred quarry, and for now she was relishing sinking her teeth into the stinking, furry mass of fox. The same soft-mouthed pup which carried her rabbits back to me alive and unharmed, had found her vocation. That drive, that singular nature, that apartness: those traits had found their release. The need to kill could now be aimed at the one animal she instinctively knew she should annihilate completely.

I hadn't yet realised it, not at that time, but the need to kill in this lurcher was so strong that it would later cause problems within our canine society. It wasn't the killing of that first fox which made the dog like this; those psychopathic seeds were sown deep in her being, from the moment she was conceived. Her 'apartness', her refusal (or was it an inability) to play games with other dogs without turning on them in furious retaliation, all these things had made her a dog apart from the rest. And whilst her dam, Seeker, hunted foxes with the determination and single-mindedness of a foxhound, she killed with no blood lust; her dispatch was clinical and simply a task to be performed as quickly and neatly as possible. To Seeker, the kill was simply the correct conclusion at the end of the hunt, the culmination of many minutes, sometimes hours, of nose work; the final act in a play, no less and no more important than all the other acts in that work.

Elka would be different. But I didn't know it at the time. I now know that there are different drives in dogs, just like the drives in an automatically-geared car. We have prey drive, fight drive and defence drive. In Elka, all three were near to the limit of what could be held in the brain of one dog. Her prey drive was massive, leading her to make extreme efforts to catch whatever she was running. But her fight drive was equal, and combined with a fierce retaliatory reaction which said: *I'm going to kill you before you can hurt me.*

Whilst some dogs that know how to take out a vicious predator can be a danger to other domestic canines as well, many good fox dogs would never dream of attacking another of their own species. Their killing drive is well contained within the strictures of canine society, and Elka too was peace personified, until another dog aggressed her. Then she became a monstrous killing force, a creature which would bear no opposition from any animal, including her fellow canines. She became, by the age of two years old, a real danger to anything which she thought had antagonised her, with the result that it was no longer safe to let her run and play with the other lurchers. Elka didn't do playing, and she never had. Until she'd found her calling in that wild and passionate killing zone, she had been safe though not sociable, around my other dogs, but once she knew how to kill, her lack of patience at the crashing play of her pack mates knew only one reaction ... to turn on that unfortunate animal and erase it from the face of the earth ... unless it was 'family'. Close relatives

60

were given the same respect and tolerance that this strange bitch afforded her owner.

Funnily enough Elka adored cats, and I don't mean that she adored killing them. She truly adored them in the way a bitch adores her puppies. Cats were sacred beings which merited both awe and tenderness combined, almost to the extent that she placed them on a pedestal. This behaviour had of course been instilled from the nest; my dogs grew up with my cats, played with them as pups, and I was fortunate in that all three cats I've owned in the past 25 years have been brilliantly assimilated into the pack. They behaved almost like honorary dogs, to the extent that they'd even come on short walks with the lurchers if I strolled up the lane behind my house.

While most lurchers are safe with 'their own' cats, many are still killers of felines unknown, but Elka refused to consider the killing of any cat, anywhere, even in the heat of the hunt on strange ground. I'll always remember how the terriers, working a spinney for fox one day, put up a large feral moggy from brambles. Elka was working loose in the wood with the terriers, and although I was some 50 metres away, on the edge of the wood with a couple of lurchers in slips, and couldn't see what was happening, I knew what the terriers had caught the moment that Elka came galloping to me. The expression on her face was extraordinary: a cardinal sin was being committed at that very moment, unseen beneath the dark pine trees. A cat was being killed! The shock was written all over the lurcher's face, ears pinned back, and her eyes were wide with the knowledge that the Cat God was being murdered behind her; she stood by my side looking as though she'd fled from a scene of unspeakable horror. I have never owned another dog which put the entire cat species upon the 'protected list', a list of animals thou shalt not kill. Elka was a strange one indeed.

~ THE SECOND FOX ~

Her second fox was found half an hour later that same day. Seeker had entered the reed bed, doing her customary foxhound impression, her nose literally dragging the ground in front of her, snuffling, reading the scent, making sure that she was moving in the right direction, the same direction as her quarry, and not following a weakening tail line as do inexperienced hunters. Her pace had quickened as she disappeared between the bone dry, crackling reed stems, though I could still see the waving fronds of the drooping seed-heads high above the dog as she pushed her way further into the invisible maze where the scent led her on.

She must have picked up speed because I faintly heard the crashing and breaking of fallen branches far out on the promontory, a beak of land jutting out into the surrounding waters of the pit. The reeds had grown first, creating a stagnant bed of silt and mud, then followed by willows, those water-loving trees which, left to their own devices, can quickly turn wet land into an island, creating out of a liquid world some higher ground which is perfect for land dwellers of all kinds. Merlin kept pace with the sounds as he galloped along the 'beach'. The beach was a gravelled strip of ground which stretched along the outer edges of the reed bed in front of me, the space between land and water, and the dog knew that his quarry should be travelling in the same direction as Seeker, though his nose, now lifting to catch the air scent, told him that the fox had leapt from its refuge and was moving fast towards the long side of the reed bed in front of him.

The flash of russet fur exploded from the reeds in front of the dog, and he fairly flew across the shifting gravel, sending sprays of small stones behind him, but wait … another lurcher, a black dog, faster and more furious by far, had overtaken Merlin, and was bearing down on the fox at impossible speed. The black dog struck the fox with a force that almost tumbled both animals into the lake, and I heard a roaring growl as the lurcher's jaws closed hard on the throat of its quarry.

As Merlin skidded to a halt beside his niece he stood back, and I gazed, amazed and shocked, as the good fox dog stood silently, panting, unable to claim his prize, for the black bitch was fixing him with blazing amber eyes filled with warning. *Back off; it's mine!* She seemed suddenly larger than before, ferocious, a force that no one could, or should defy.

It might sound fanciful, but Elka's eyes fairly glowed with an inner light, a demon unleashed in the young and inexperienced animal. We waited in silence and Seeker, as she emerged from the reeds, panting and stained with black mud, stood back too, respectful and somehow diminished in form beside that of her daughter.

And then, as quickly as the demon had appeared, it vanished, and Elka was Elka again, now tiring of defending 'her' fox from the others, and although she still kept her grip on the now lifeless carcase, her body language must have subtly changed for both dam and uncle laid hold of the fox in order to claim their part in the hunt.

I used to think that Elka was simply one of those dogs with an over-active defence mechanism, a kind of "I'm going to kill you before you hurt me" attitude, but as she hadn't been bitten by either of those first two foxes this theory was blown out of the water. Her desire to kill was purely instinctual; her ability to read the intentions of her quarry had been born of those genes passed down from her ancestors which recognised that different quarry needed different tactics.

Was she a true psychopath? Her inability to interact with other dogs led me to believe so initially, but that label alone wasn't correct. She wasn't dangerous to other dogs just so long as they left her alone ... at first. And like the Mafiosa, it was all about FAMILY! She'd play with Seeker, and later her half sister, brought into the pack when Elka was about four years old, and she behaved in a positively flirtatious manner around some male dogs, but not all. Canines outside her immediate blood relatives were tolerated so long as they kept their distance. For the most part she simply wanted to be left alone, and her days, whilst not hunting, were spent waiting to hunt. It was all she lived for.

Whilst she was quietly affectionate towards me, she never went out of her way to demonstrate that affection. We might share a glance across the room at home, and if I looked at her, she was always aware, turning those strange, searchlight eyes to mine the moment she felt my gaze upon her. She might lean against my leg if we stopped when out mooching, but hated being hugged or any other silly human demonstrations of love. She was contained and contented in her world, so long as she was left alone.

She seemed to have that extra lethal gene, that ability, and more importantly, the desire and need, to kill fast and efficiently, but dammit, she also enjoyed that power. She revelled in her own ferocity, and an instinct from time immemorial to deal death to foxes. Was this a breed trait, handed down from her Beardie forbears ... those tough and independent herders of sheep who must defend their flock against predators? Or had she just inherited a combination of genetic traits which loved the kill? In which case, why was she so soft-mouthed on game that didn't bite back?

Later Elka added muntjac and hare to her list of obtainable quarry, though she didn't have the gears to catch strong fen hares on a regular basis; her all-or-nothing blast of speed and her insane need to catch led her to overshoot the canny hares we encountered on the open fens. She soon burned herself out on such courses and she never ran them frequently enough to gain the sort of understanding that makes a good hare dog. Had she been brought up on the fens with very regular exposure to this type of game, I've no doubt that she'd have learned a few tricks, though she'd never have possessed that out-and-out marathon runner's stamina we see in the Saluki-saturated hounds.

She didn't fare too well in her exploits on muntjac either, never learning the need for prudence when it came to throat holding those tusked and horned 'wood pigs'. Her smash and grab style often left her ripped and torn, and she failed to realise that a back-of-the-neck hold wasn't wise when the muntjac could throw back its head to gouge its attacker with those sharp little horns.

Elka's work wasn't faultless, and I hated taking her digging with the terriers because she couldn't wait patiently and quietly whilst the terrier fought long and unseen battles below ground. The normally silent bitch couldn't bear to hear and feel those vibrations seeping up through the earth while she stood by, inactive, frustrated. In short, she was a right royal pain to take foxing and I only took her if there was an extra pair of hands to hang on to her collar to stop her from pacing backwards and forwards or digging desperately to get into the earth. No terrier was going to have all that fun whilst she stood by idle.

Years later I realised that if she was allowed to find an occupied earth for herself, the whining and pacing behaviour she'd previously displayed simply vanished. When she found an earth thus, she stood patiently, well back from the entrance, whilst the terrier attempted to bolt the occupant. In other words, she then felt in control of the situation because it was she that had found the earth. It was her event to work as she wanted.

~ THE FOX ON THE CLIFF ~

I really realised just how determined Elka was when she went on a fox that Seeker had pushed from some brambles along the edge of an old gravel pit. She'd have been around two years old at the time, and the gravel pits were now abandoned, leaving great scars of raw sand and earth over what had once been farm land. I'd never known this land as grass fields, for when I first arrived in the area back in the 1980s the ground was already being torn up in the search for the gravel which lay just beneath the surface.

We walked on the tracks left by the huge machines which toiled to extract the gravel, though some of the pits were old and disused, already in the process of becoming the lakes we see today. Around the oldest abandoned pits grew brambles, the first plants of nature's army to reclaim the land; they climbed and clung to the steep cliffs and banks, pushing their roots deep into the crumbling soil, anchoring the earth and providing the wildlife with places to hide.

Seeker had found a fox along one such cliff face. I call it a cliff, though most were less than ten metres in height, but these walls of sand and clay were sheer, and not easy for dogs to negotiate. Seeker had managed to follow the scent along the side of one such wall, slipping and climbing amongst the brambles, and she'd bolted the fox, unseen by the other dogs. Only Elka, ahead of the rest, anticipating events with her usual awareness and zeal, caught a glimpse as a red furry flash showed itself briefly on the track, before disappearing down the next cliff and into the old gravel pit. She took off in pursuit, a vain hope, I thought at the time.

I ran, hollering the rest of the dogs on, though I never expected them to catch up with the fox, which would surely be long gone and into the next swathe of cover alongside the fishing lakes. As

I arrived at the spot where I'd seen Elka jump from the track and into the pit, I looked across the empty space to the opposite cliff to where I thought she might have gone, but saw nothing. The ground dropped away beneath my feet, a yawning hole which looked like a moonscape or a battleground from the First World War.

The whole pit was one vast area of deep trenches and gouges from the tracks of machines long since working elsewhere, and in the middle was a small lake, gradually filling the pit with water which seeped from the surrounding land. The whole scene was one of complete devastation, a testament to man's ability to destroy the land. Today, nearly 20 years later, when I look out over the water surrounded by willows and reeds, I find it hard to believe that nature has so perfectly reclaimed this place: it is a calm and beautiful lake, filled with water birds of all kinds. Swans, coots and moorhens scatter the water, and in winter there are flocks of teal and wigeon, not to mention the geese. Snowy egrets visit often, and I've even disturbed bitterns as they stand like invisible sentries among the reeds.

I stood with the rest of the dogs waiting for Elka to return, and then I saw a movement at the edge of the brambles on the far side of the pit ... Elka pushed her way out of the cover, and she was carrying the fox. She stopped on the edge of the ten metre drop, and then did something I've never witnessed before or since: she deliberately dropped the carcase off the edge of the cliff, obviously realising that to attempt the leap carrying something quite heavy could be dangerous. Quick as a flash she scrabbled down the steep clay wall and even before the fox had stopped rolling downwards, grabbed it once more in her jaws, and began to carry it across the floor of the pit towards me.

But she needed a drink, and instead of coming straight to me, she dropped into the pool which lay to one side of her path. She swam into the middle of the pool, let go of the fox and trod water, happily drinking and cooling herself, the fox floating lifelessly nearby! I really thought she'd leave it floating when she came out of the pool, but after almost forgetting it, Elka turned and picked up her burden once more.

She carried that fox all the way to me, clambering awkwardly up the steep cliff at my feet, and laid it on the ground before me, shook herself hard, and looked at her dam, then at me, as if to say: *'There you go! I got it!'* That was Elka all over. She continually astonished me with the way she did things. That was the only time she actually retrieved a fox to me, and I think that she did so because she had caught far from my sight.

~ A GOOD DOG DAY WITH SEEKER AND ELKA ~

One day, after the end of the shooting season, we'd been invited on to an estate in Lincolnshire many miles from our usual haunts. Flat land, huge fields bisected by drains, those large drainage ditches dug out by man to render the fen swamps suitable for cultivation. We'd made our way to an earth which was set on the side of a drain, at a T-junction of drains. There were three entrances to this earth, one leading out to the cut-away bank of one drain, almost at field level, high above any potential flooding, and another, situated about a metre below the first, almost at flood water level, though now dry and inviting. The third exit, for this was an exit as opposed to an entrance, was a tiny hole in the adjoining drain, an escape in times of need. We took up our stations around the earth. The gamekeeper stood, gun at the ready, in the bottom of the drain, whilst I held Elka, restrained and impatient, on the edge of the field above.

Seeker was allowed to use her own judgement as to where she placed herself and as usual she stayed on top of the field where her view-point was best. The terrier crept from sight into the earth. Merlin was with us as well, standing guard near the entrance the terrier had used, but standing well back from view should a fox stick its nose into the daylight prior to making its escape.

When you stand waiting like this, for moments, they seem like hours. All is quiet, save for the rustling of dry sedge grass along the dyke side, and even Elka was silent for once, a welcome change from her usual breathy whining when waiting for a fox to bolt. I had hold of her collar though. It always makes sense to keep one dog back in these situations as you never know how many foxes an earth might hold.

Then it happens, and from one second to the next, the silence and stillness is shattered into a host of different noises. The shout, though the exact words are never remembered later; then the crack from the rifle, and another, then curses. He'd missed!

A fox has bolted from the bottom exit in the main drain, but instead of leaping up on to the field, it has taken a sharp left into the adjoining drain bottom, and it is running flat out along a ledge which acts like a path for the wild animals which use the drains and dykes as safe roads whereby they can keep themselves hidden below the level of the land, hidden from the sight of those who walk the land.

The fox is running away along this path, and presented with a small, rapidly receding target, the game keeper's bullets have failed to connect. Andy leaps the dyke calling Seeker to him, and although she's not even seen the fox leave the earth, she canters alongside the man, pulled on by the urgency in his voice, and she's bouncing, wondering what's happening. Then she catches the scent of the running fox; scent which wafts up from the dyke, and washes over her in waves as she runs.

She goes down a gear and now she's galloping hard along the edge of the field, unsighted on her quarry, and although the fox is almost a hundred yards in front of her, she is gaining ... and still gaining. Now a dot so far away, a moving dark shape against the green expanse of winter wheat ... still gaining, until she disappears into the dyke, and comes out on top again, hard on the heels of the fox.

She's run on that air scent wafting up from the dyke until she's come level with the fox, or rather, she's known that the fox has been overhauled, and she'd leapt down to intercept her quarry.

Seeker's only a small bitch, dead on 23 inches, and despite her ability to find and kill foxes in cover, she's never been brilliant at taking them on top on the run. It can turn into a running battle, and sometimes she's reluctant to tackle them at a gallop. The strange thing is that she'll draw them all day long, despite the punishment they dish out. I know where this reluctance stems from, because as a young dog of only 18 months, she came up against a huge dog fox in a beet field, which managed to get its jaws round the skull of the dog. It was a mad situation, where the fox was unable to release its grip, jaws forced too wide to relinquish that hold, and I'd had to pry its teeth loose with a spade having dispatched the creature. Even in death the jaws had remained fixed in the head of the young lurcher.

It took four full years for Seeker to overcome that experience, though eventually she learned some manoeuvres to outsmart her quarry. Even so, she was never as good as her daughter and granddaughter when taking fox in the open.

Now she's jinking and twisting, barging the fox, but we can hardly see details at this distance, over 200 yards, and Andy's still running towards the two animals, and then comes Merlin, out of the dyke like a big brindle wolf from its lair. He's followed the line of the fox along the dyke side, trailing behind his target, following it by sight, though struggling on the steep bank sides on a path made for foxes by foxes, not large dogs.

Merlin ploughs in and flips the fox, and both dogs settle on their chosen holds: Seeker on the throat, and the more powerful dog on the ribs. The whole bolt, run and kill has probably taken just over a minute, though as we stand, us humans, rooted to the spot, helpless bystanders to a battle which needs no intervention from us, our minds are already replaying the action, and we almost forget that the terrier is still to ground, and going hard at it by the sound of incessant baying that we hear, once we've settled down again.

No time to settle for long for there's another shout, and a second fox has bolted from the tiny bolt hole on the adjoining dyke side: and I slip Elka. She hasn't seen it go from where she stands, up on the field well back from the drain, but she knows; she's reading our human body language as accurately as though we'd been dogs. Instinctively we all move in the direction the fox has taken as it runs low, scudding along the bottom of the dry dyke.

Elka and I leap into the dyke at the same instant. She, to run up alongside the fox, me to see what is happening! I see the dog overhaul the fox in quick strides, and you know how certain images imprint themselves on your memory, fixed there for ever. Like a camera shutter, my eye takes snap shots of the action; my mind stores them for ever.

The dog seems to run straight past the fox, but at the last moment, when the two are level, she twists her head sideways, down and then up again, and she's got the fox by the throat and it's under her body, legs thrashing against hers. The keeper runs up and puts a bullet in its head. I curse him silently, knowing how quickly a dog can change its grip or lose its footing during the heat of battle. I needn't have worried. He's not a fool, or a trigger-happy novice, but the action still scares me. Guns and dogs don't always mix and I've seen good dogs shot by fools when the guns have exceeded their remit. Almost as though they don't want to, can't be left out of the kill, won't allow the dog to take all the credit. Guns do strange things to some people. Sometimes it's just too dangerous to intervene whilst a dog is fast to its quarry; though of course there is also the need to despatch the quarry as fast as possible; humanely.

No true hunter would ever want to stand by and observe a prolonged battle between dog and prey; no right-minded person would enjoy seeing either dog or fox in pain. Dogs which take a good throat hold are the best. It is possible to step in and administer the coup de grace with no risk to the dog. Dogs which grab a fox in the guts or by a hind leg and shake like fury are both dangerous to themselves and also prolong a fox's agony unnecessarily.

A big strong dog can break a fox's back with a couple of shakes if it knows what it is doing, but the throat hold immobilises the fox instantly. Of course, a dog which only takes its quarry by the throat will lose foxes, that much is true, and the best dogs are, in my opinion, those which throat their prey, but are prepared to take a bite when needed in their jousting to get that hold.

But even the throat dog's way isn't without danger, as this next account will reveal.

~ THE DROWNING ~

Elka took many foxes during her lifetime, both by day and by night on the lamp. And she did learn to avoid those teeth, except when retaliation was unavoidable. Rather than see a fox reach cover, and possible escape, she'd strike out desperately and grab the brush of a fleeing fox as it neared the safety of brambles. She knew full well that she'd suffer the consequences; that the fox

Opposite: The same river, serene in the sunlight.

70

would spin round and close its dagger teeth on her muzzle, but to her, this was infinitely preferable to seeing it escape.

The following events took place one cold November night many years ago, long before the shooters had adopted night vision goggles, and our local foxes were still relatively uneducated in the ways of lamps and man. The air was almost at freezing temperature, and our breath puffed out in white clouds before us at every step. The air was almost still, with barely a breeze to ruffle the calm of that welcome darkness which we lampers yearn for during the too-long days at work.

We knew exactly where we'd find foxes, but whether or not we'd get within reach of them on a night so still and calm remained to be seen. We knew also that the best field for foxes, a field of set-aside, had just been topped. The first night after a harvest or cut often seems to confuse the local wildlife. It's almost as though they don't realise that their cover has gone. Both muntjac and fox wander aimlessly across the open land as though they are still hidden from sight by standing crops or weeds. By the following night they've realised that some serious changes have

Elka.

72

been wrought to their habitat! For the third fox in this account, that realisation would never come.

Picture a gently undulating pasture, flanked to the left by an old railway line, dotted with trees and bushes. To the right lies the tributary of a river, hidden from view as it carves its sluggish way between the grassy banks. Over many years, the river has cut a deep path through the pasture-land, and along the sloping banks which follow the river's contours are the paths cut by animals. Sheep and cattle, muntjac and foxes use these paths, which form one continuous ledge you can't see when you stand at a distance from the water.

We are standing, Andy and I, with our backs to the old railway line, scanning the field. I spot a pair of yellow eyes at about 120 yards, and the eyes are snuffed out almost as soon as the beam identifies the blurred shape of a fox. I do something totally daft, something I'd never do now, and something so unlikely to succeed that only an idiot would expect a result. But back then, I had a bitch called Elka at my side, and the faint breeze has lifted the scent to the dog. I slipped her, knowing she'd seen those eyes too, and I kept the beam on the dog as she sped towards where the golden orbs had shone for all too brief a second in time. Then she vanished, and I saw nothing more.

What prompted me to run towards the river? What instinct made me turn to my right, to light up the bank behind me? I might have heard the thudding feet of a dog as it passed me, unseen, but I'd seen nothing at all in the light of the beam. I stood and waited, played the beam back across the field just in case the dog had gone to the left. Still nothing ... then a weird sort of cry, a half strangled yelp, then a splash. I ran faster, and frantically played the beam up and down the bank, from left to right, and back again. Nothing, no fox, no dog, not a sign or a sound from either.

My guts started to twist in fear and foreboding. My heart hammered dully as I imagined the impossible, and I shone the beam directly into the river. The impossible was happening. There, beneath the green and glassy surface of the sluggish river surface I could clearly see the dog and the fox, sinking ever deeper into the icy depths of the river. Jaw to jaw they sank, unmoving, like two dead beasts, and I screamed for Andy to get over to me.

This is where the whole night became slightly surreal, and at the risk of making light of subsequent events, there followed an insane few moments which will be forever engraved in my mind, almost as though it were yesterday's action.

I screamed, "Andy, save her!" Strange how the mighty hunter, when faced with a potential tragedy of such awesome proportions, dissolves into little woman freaking out at the thought of her dog's death! I still blush to think of my pathetic plea to this day! Andy never hesitated, he jumped straight off the bank into the river ... and found himself up to his chest in the water. Feet slipping on the oozing mud, he scanned the surrounding depths, looking for signs of the animals.

Then up popped the fox, not two feet before him, and it swam straight at him, snapping at his face: don't forget, one moment it had been battling the dog, then nearly drowned, so now it was still in defence mode, determined to battle it out to the last.

And then I saw Elka surface, further out in the middle of the river, and she swam, disorientated and cold, in the wrong direction, away from us, making for the far bank, where a curious crowd of bovine spectators had gathered ... a herd of cattle, summoned by the unusual disturbance to their ruminant sleep, were starting to push and shove each other in simple curiosity. That was all the poor dog needed! I switched my attention back to the drama unfolding at my feet, and as the fox swam at Andy, he reached over its head and grabbed its scruff, and attempted to pass it up to me. I reached and grabbed, and felt the slippery wet fur slide through my fingers. Splosh went the fox, back into the water. Andy grabbed it again, and this time I lassoed it with a rope dog lead and dragged it on to the bank to despatch it.

By this time Elka had realised, despite her near drowning, that she was on the wrong side of the water, and she was being nudged by the curious herd of young stock. They jostled and pushed in their attempt to analyse this intruder on the edge of their field, though luckily with no real aggression. I called to the dog, waving her frantically towards me, and after a second's hesitation, she leapt back into the freezing dark water and swam to me. I scruffed her and dragged her up on to the bank, and although she was now shivering so badly that she could barely stand up, she launched a ferocious attack on the carcase as soon as she felt her feet on dry land.

"Well, help me out then!" came Andy's voice from the river, and he too was lassoed with the dog lead and I hauled him out! Actually, he grabbed hold of the loop in the rope, and pulled himself up the bank whilst I leaned back and prayed that his weight wouldn't land me in the river as well! Water poured from every pocket of his waxed coat; his boots were, amazingly, still on his feet despite the suction of the mud, but best of all, his lamp was still working. Full of water, with small specks of duckweed floating past the glass, that lamp was working: unbelievable!

Andy spent the next few moments emptying his boots, wringing out his socks, turning out his pockets: his wallet was now a soggy mess of notes and receipts: that would have to wait for later.

"Do you want to go home?" I asked him.

"I'm wet now. We might as well carry on", he replied, shivering almost as much as the dog. My admiration for him knew no bounds! I also figured that if Elka could run a couple of rabbits she'd start to warm up a bit.

We crossed the field and the railway line to the next pasture where we knew there'd be rabbits. I spotted one, and Elka went out, turned it twice, struck and retrieved it live to hand. She was still shivering uncontrollably. I'd never run a cold, wet dog nowadays. It's a recipe for injury. Ah, the ignorant bliss of youth, combined with the enthusiasm and the knowledge that there might be more foxes out there in the dark.

Then Andy spotted another bunny far out in the field, a rabbit which he knew would head for the far side of that pasture. He walked out, past the rabbit, in order to lamp it back in to the hedge. Keki was nearly seven years old and very experienced on the lamp. He put that rabbit away in double quick time, but as he retrieved his squealing catch to his master, a dark shape ran in towards man and dog. Another fox!

Now Keki never had been, never would be a fox dog, but for some strange reason he gave chase to this fox. Round and round the field they went, dodging and darting, jousting and twisting, whilst Elka and I stood transfixed on the side lines. Should I slip her or not? The distance was too great, I thought. The fox would make it to the far hedge before she could get on terms.

Elka was never overly demonstrative.

As I watched, the fox came back into the middle of the field. No seasoned veteran this, but a first year youngster, panicked and confused. It ran straight at Andy, and between his legs! Keki struck from the side as the fox made to gallop away. Was he encouraged to see fox as prey after watching Elka: he'd seen her take fox on the lamp on previous nights? I'll never know what went through his head on this night, and I slipped Elka ... I had to. Poor Keki would surely come off worst, unused to biting quarry. Elka all but killed the fox on the first strike, piling into it like a missile. We watched her rag the carcase ferociously.

"Let's go home now", I said, for Andy was still shivering; he was soaked to the skin and now the river mist was beginning to creep across the field in a chill white layer.

We walked back along the railway line, and just a few moments had passed before I just couldn't help but play the beam out across the field to our right. And there was another fox! A big, yellowish fox, trotting steadily along the fence line, not 50 yards from where we stood. Had it heard the rabbit squeal a few moments before? It seemed focused and intent.

Between fox and hunters lay a wide, rushy ditch, then a fence of barbed wire. I slipped Elka, and she leapt the ditch, then the wire, and closed with the fox as I clambered after her, trying to keep the beam steady as I crawled over the fence. The fox was only ten metres from a big bramble in the corner of the field when Elka reached it. Her quarry put on a spurt of speed, realising the danger ... too late. The dog put in a desperate strike and grabbed the fox's brush, and he swung round and clamped sharp teeth on the lurcher's head. This was no first season fox, but a veteran of countless battles with its own kind. It was one of the biggest foxes I'd seen in this area, and an odd honey colour, far paler than the normal rust red hue of Vulpes vulpes.

The night air was split with the sound of the dog's howls, and the next moment I saw Keki tear past me and bowl into the fox with a vengeance that left Andy and I both open-mouthed. I saw Elka, now free of the fox, back off, then strike again, miss, and end up again with her jaws between those of her foe. Cold and tired, her reactions were not what they should have been, and again Keki moved in, and locked his own jaws on the throat of the fox. I couldn't believe what I was seeing. This was a dog that had never before in his life attempted to engage a fox. He just ignored them if he saw them in the beam. He was a rabbit dog, pure and simple, and a damn good rabbit dog at that. But a fox dog? Never!

By the time we got to the scene of battle it was nearly all over. Both dogs had gained the upper hand, two sets of jaws firmly on the throat of their foe.

Elka wasn't a pretty sight. Her muzzle streamed with blood from several deep gashes, and she looked truly exhausted, for the first time in her life. She was still almost hypothermic after her immersion in that frigid water not 40 minutes before. But her tail still wagged slowly in satisfaction. We went home.

I dried off my lurcher, and washed her head carefully, noting the deep puncture wounds and slashes along the length of her muzzle and under her jaw. I dripped antibiotic ointment into the wounds, and she never moved nor winced nor showed any other

sign of pain. She then wolfed down a meal fit for a king, while Andy carefully spread the soggy notes and cards from his wallet along the radiator to dry.

Keki did have one more attempt on a fox, several weeks later, but got nipped on the nose and backed off, never to engage such quarry again. I am firmly convinced that he went to Elka's aid in her time of need, spurred on by her howls of pain. There could be no other reason for his kamikaze actions, so out of character in one such as him.

Apart from the manic sequence of events that night, one crazy snap shot stands out in my memory. That of the lamp, bulb aglow behind the duckweed and water that filled the casing, like some tiny back lit aquarium. All it would have needed was a tiny fish to complete the illusion!

Elka met her death whilst running a muntjac through treacherous woodland, sustaining serious internal injuries when she hit a wooden fence overgrown with brambles and weeds. She was a dog in a million. The perfect catch dog. The perfect killing machine. The perfect fox dog. She was only seven years old at the time of her death.

I have seen her run fox through a flock of sheep, ignoring all but the quarry before her, when her target tried to use the woolly bodies to disguise its tracks and scent. I have seen her crash headlong into a dense mass of bramble, tearing ears and face on thorny stems in order to reach her prey. And I've seen her carefully retrieving a rabbit, with jaws as gentle as those of a mother crocodile carrying its young to the river. And just as those same jaws are capable of crushing and killing, so did Elka's jaws have the capacity to kill with the same ferocity as those of a crocodile.

You don't realise just how good a dog you have until you have lesser dogs with which to compare them. I now know that Elka was a very good dog indeed.

Ready to bolt.

~ Angel ~

Angel was Elka's daughter, from a mating to a small, tough dog from a predominantly Bedlington-Whippet line of lurchers. Lurchers can look like their parents, or they can look nothing alike at all. Elka was rough coated, black, and around 24 inches; Angel was smooth, blue, and looked a bit like a heavily built Whippet. To my shame and great sadness, I don't have a single photo of this bitch, apart from one taken by a friend when she was a pup. For many years I didn't own a camera myself, so most of the photos I have of my dogs from the earlier years were taken by friends during a day's hunting, or even more occasionally at home.

Most of Angel's siblings were mini-Elkas in appearance, and once again, Angel was the pup that nobody wanted ... except me. I don't know why I chose this unremarkable pup from a litter of classy, rough-coated beauties. But I did choose her, quite early on in her life, when she was only about six weeks of age. To be honest, there were several smooth pups at this stage, though all but Angel went on to sprout thick rough coats by the time they were a year old. Angel stayed almost as smooth as a Greyhound though her coat was thicker, more like that of a smooth Collie.

I've often noticed that lurchers don't exhibit their adult coats until 12 months or older. Elka herself was smooth until she was ten months of age, but as Angel matured she kept her smooth coat, something I think helped her slide through cover so easily. I've often noticed that the really rough-coated lurchers aren't so keen to get tangled in briars as the smooth dogs I've owned.

Whilst looks might be important, I have always chosen a pup by instinct. Well, nearly always! On the odd occasion where I've been swayed by coat colour or type, I've come a cropper, big time! I need to rely on gut instinct when picking a pup, no matter how shy, how small or how ugly that pup might be. Ugly? What is ugly to one person might be heaven on earth to another, and I've picked some oddities in my time, which later became swans indeed if I'm talking about their prowess in the field.

Angel as a pup, and sadly, the only photo I have of the dynamic little bitch.

Angel matured to just under 22 inches in height; she was quiet, unobtrusive, and happy with her place in the world. She was an out-and-out nose dog, like her grand-dam Seeker, and what a nose it was! I can remember one of the first rabbits she found, at around six months of age ...

The terriers had checked out a fallen pile of branches, and moved on. (Even terriers can get it wrong sometimes!) Little Angel stayed put, refusing to come away. I went back to the pup, who was glaring fixedly into the dense heap of branches, then pushing and shoving her way in to find the source of a scent that she knew lay hidden, deep in the twisted pile of wood. Not only did she find that rabbit, but she caught it too, with a scream of delight as she blasted the branches aside and deftly grabbed her prize by one hind leg. Then she had to retrieve it, which took some time, for she was trapped in a cage of twigs and debris.

I like to let pups work out for themselves how to deal with obstacles in the field, and I watched as the pup first pulled, then pushed the rabbit through the maze, until she could finally free both herself and her catch, and place it at my feet. That gleeful scream as she lunged for the rabbit? Yup, Angel was a screamer ... that most hideous of sins in a lurcher. She yapped when running through cover, and she screamed like a banshee if she didn't catch her rabbit on the first turn out in the open. Did I care? Not one bit! I tried her on the lamp, but couldn't stand the noise, so I used her to her strengths ... in cover.

No cover was too dense, no bramble too thick. If there was something which needed to be flushed or caught, then Angel did it, and her small size gave her a great advantage over the larger lurchers. And for Angel, just like her mother and grandmother before her, it was foxes that really rocked Angel's boat. Her Beardie forebears gave her a tough, thick skin; the Bedlington from the sire's line gave her that terrier toughness and grit to see the job through to the end, and the running dog input gave her the speed to run down a fox in the open. More importantly, she'd inherited those particular genes from countless generations of dogs which were doing the job in the field, regardless of the exact percentage of this breed or that.

She might have been little, but her incredible agility and drive equalled the odds when it came to tackling a quarry sometimes not a lot smaller than herself. Of course any fox would, in truth, be smaller than Angel, but they look a lot bigger than they really are when they are up and running. Only in death do they seem to shrink to their true size, for death makes all of us smaller, humans and animals alike. Once the spirit has left the physical body there is no longer a life force to hold the flesh strong and proud.

Angel was strong too, with a well-muscled neck and powerful, though diminutive jaws. People sometimes make the mistake of thinking that the bite of a small lurcher is too weak to deal death to foxes. Make no mistake, even a Whippet has the jaw power to kill a fox: it is more down to skill and having that particular knack than anything else, though a lot of Whippets are too gung-ho for their own good ... throwing caution to the winds when you've got skin like tissue paper isn't always a good idea.

Angel's skin was as tough as her mind; and just as well, or her hide would have been criss-crossed with scars long before she hit 12 months of age. As it was, her muzzle soon bore faint lines of white scar tissue, and her ears frequently ended up bound to her head with masses of Vetwrap after those desperate dives into brambles. She frequently emerged from a kill drenched in her own blood, and come to me panting and happy, scarlet of head and ears, the blood streaming from deep gouges through the tender skin of her ear flaps, testimony to her manic determination through the brambles.

You always remember the first fox a dog takes, on its own. Like a rite of passage, that moment in time stays with you forever, engraved in the memory like a tiny, stained glass window, complete with colours and details etched sharp in your mind. Subsequent kills might blur and intermingle with others, but the first one stays true.

Angel's first fox was taken deep in a bramble, a fortress of thorny boughs too tightly woven for larger lurchers to enter. And I could do nothing to help the little blue bitch as she battled her foe in its depths. I needn't have worried, for Angel's instinct to go for the throat and suffocate her prey was inbuilt and perfect.

Unlike her grandma, Seeker, who, as a youngster, tended to relinquish her grip on her adversary's throat once it went limp, with sometimes surprising consequences (anyone who has hunted foxes will know that they can seem dead, only to get up and run off the moment they feel themselves free), Angel somehow knew from the beginning that she had to increase that grip, only relaxing her jaws enough to bite deeper into her quarry. And she knew that she had to maintain that vice-like hold until the heart of her prey had stopped beating altogether. She never made a mistake, not even on that first solo fox.

~ THE FOX BETWEEN THE WALLS ~

One of Angel's finer moments came about when we were digging on the fens. We'd found traces of fox round a small grain store set in the middle of nowhere, out on the flat lands of a farm we patrolled on a regular basis. Next to the grain store, only 50 metres away, lay a small dew pond, surrounded by banks which were riddled with rabbit holes, then a mess of small bushes and trees.

I need to explain the construction of the grain store, because you'll see that the details are all important in this tale ... the building was constructed from concrete blocks, up to a height of around eight feet. The top part of the wall was made from box metal sheets, which came down from the roof to just overlap the concrete wall.

The walls were double-skinned, the inner wall being made of exterior ply, leaving a gap of around ten inches in width, between the outer concrete wall and the inner wooden cladding. There were two large doors to the store, situated on adjacent sides of the building, and whilst the gap between the skins was blocked with wood to accommodate the hinges of one door, there was no such block next to the other door, which left a narrow tunnel leading between the two walls, albeit a tunnel with only one exit. Anything going into that gap had only one way out, which would be the same way it went in.

The building was in good repair, apart from a hole in the metal cladding just above the concrete wall, near to the main door, a hole probably made when a farm worker had backed a fork lift or similar into the wall, leaving a jagged tear to the sheet, a hole which a terrier would have been hard pushed to get into, had it been able to fly up eight feet in the first place! Now that I've got this necessary, if boring, explanation out of the way, read on and find out why the structure of this wall was to be so important in this tale ...

The terrier started showing an interest in one of the rabbit holes round the pond and eventually she scrabbled her way into the warren. Less than a minute later out came a fox, too fast for reaction, a small vixen by the look of it. We hadn't netted up; there were too many holes, besides which, we hadn't really expected a fox to have taken up residence in a rabbit warren. Some people never learn! Foxes are often found in the most unlikely of places.

The fox dashed round the corner of the grain store and vanished, closely followed by Angel, who also vanished, seemingly into thin air. What the hell? Then came the banging and scuffling and I knew what had happened. The reason I knew the layout of the store so well was because it had formed part of my monthly pest control rounds for some years, before a back injury forced me out of that occupation. I'd positioned bait boxes as far up the tunnel as I could reach with a long stick, balancing the box on the point of the stick before laying it deep in the tunnel. I also knew that there wasn't an exit at the far end of the tunnel.

I realised that Angel and fox were both trapped in the end of the gap between the two walls of the store. The fox had fled into the dark, narrow sanctuary, and had come up against the timber which blocked the exit. Through a tiny, very tiny, chink between wood and block, I could just see the dog, on top of the fox, and she'd pinned it with her normal efficiency. There was nothing we could do except wait for Angel to finish her job, and hope she'd have the sense to turn round or back out of the tunnel in the way she'd gone in.

Then the truly surreal happened. One moment we were standing next to the wall, the next we saw a flash of red explode through the broken sheeting above the concrete wall, and a fox sailed over our heads and hit the ground running. Open mouthed, we gawped at the fox as it disappeared round the ponds and banks in the direction of the set aside field; then someone put eye to chink and told us that Angel was still in the tunnel, still finishing off her fox, but not for long ... seconds later a blue blur executed the same crazy manoeuvre, leaping over our heads and galloped off, nose to ground, in pursuit of that second fox.

She followed the line at a gallop until she lost the scent in a vast field of set aside, several hundred yards away, and eventually returned panting, but none too down-hearted. I lunged at the bitch as she came past me, and grabbed her for she seemed intent on getting back into the tunnel to vent her disappointment on the carcase. We managed to verify that the first fox was indeed dead, through the judicious application of gravel thrown down through the hole in the wall on to the carcase: no reaction. Besides which, it would have to be a cold day in hell for Angel to leave a fox alive.

I will never knowingly leave any prey, be it vermin or otherwise, injured. This is one of my principles. If you kill animals, you must do it as efficiently and humanely as possible. I don't have a problem with sensible guns at all, but at the risk of upsetting one of the largest field sports fraternities in the country, far too many shooters are content to blast away when in truth they are out of killing range, and this seems to apply particularly to foxes, which are considered vermin by most right-minded country folk. That these shots are taken with the full knowledge that the animal will probably die a lingering death over several days only makes this act more reprehensible.

In my opinion, there is NEVER any excuse or reason not to ensure that the animal you kill does indeed die as swiftly as is possible.

Whilst the anti-dog brigade wring their hands in horror at the thought of dogs killing foxes, at least a dog kills outright, within seconds. Well, good dogs kill quickly at any rate. Not so good dogs are unlikely to do a fox much damage at all if they're scared of the pointy end of the beast.

We checked again on the fox as it lay unmoving at the end of the tunnel between the shed walls, definitely dead, no movement from ribs, and although it was hardly proper to leave it there to rot down and infect the surrounding area with that noxious, dead thing smell, we couldn't figure out a way to extricate it without committing some major structural damage to the building. Pest control may be one thing, but a substantial hole in the side of the barn was another.

Now, the thing which really intrigues me is this: obviously there were two foxes in the tunnel, one which bolted into the gap and one which must have already been there. Angel must have squeezed up that tunnel and dealt death to the one, whilst the other, trapped at the end, eventually managed to climb up the wall and out through the hole in the sheeting. The fact that Angel was able to do the same, meant that she must have wiggled up the wall, a bit like a chimney sweep in olden times, bracing her back against one wall, whilst 'walking' up the opposite side of the tunnel.

To do this, and then scrape her way out through a gap in the sheeting, which didn't look to be large enough to accommodate my two hands laid side by side, and all without damage to herself, was feat enough, and bearing in mind that she'd just been battered about in the space between the walls in her encounter ... t'was pretty amazing. I think back on that day now, and I'm still amazed by both the determination and sheer ability of that bitch.

Interestingly enough, where Seeker drew foxes, Elka refused ever to push into an earth. She couldn't stand to feel trapped. Angel, however, had inherited her grand-dam's love of dark places, and like Seeker, would push on to the stop end to lend the terrier a hand at the end of a dig.

It is politically incorrect to even mention a draw dog in this day and age, where everything has to be 'humanely dispatched' with a gun. In theory, it's a bit of a touchy subject to even mention digging a fox out: they have to be 'flushed' to a gun and the only time you're allowed to dig is to free a trapped terrier. But I'm not speaking of nowadays, and then, when I actually did terrier work on a regular basis, it was the norm to use a good drawing dog to bring an end to the matter if the fox wouldn't bolt or you'd dug down a little too short, leaving a couple of yards to the stop end. If you had a lurcher which would enter the tube and crawl forward to get to grips with the fox, it made life a lot easier, and the end a lot quicker for the quarry. It also saved the terrier a fair bit of grief, and both Seeker and Angel would feel their way carefully alongside the terrier until they could get a good grip of their prey's head, before bracing their feet against the walls of the tunnel and pulling it out.

~ ONLY THE GOOD DIE YOUNG ~

Seeker, Elka and Angel, three generations of tough, multi-tasking lurchers, and they all died before they were eight years of age.

Seeker died in her sleep a few weeks short of her eighth birthday, after a massive hunt on either a muntjac or fox. I never knew if she'd killed her quarry, for the hunt took her across two rivers, a flood plain and into a wood. On her eventual return to my side, she had seemed exhausted and cold, but ate her supper just fine, and rested in front of the fire for the evening. When I woke the next morning she was dead, lying at the foot of our bed as though still asleep. I'd heard a muffled squeaking during the night, which half woke me from sleep, and thinking she'd been dreaming, had stuck my foot out of the end of the bed and stroked her with my toes, and thought no more of it.

I never had a post mortem done. I couldn't have born the thought of her body, flayed and lifeless, lying cold on the vet's examining table. Besides which, dissection wouldn't have brought her back to me: dead is dead. My own thoughts on the matter, and those of my vet, to whom I relayed the details, were that a blood clot, an embolism, had entered her heart, blocking those intricate valves and pipes, bringing an end to the life of one of the best little lurchers I've known. I was privileged to have owned her, and still prouder to have born witness to the work she did during those eight years of life.

Elka made it to seven years old, as I've already said, and I feel no guilt at the manner of her passing, for the accident which killed her was just that, an unavoidable accident of the sort that do-or-die dogs run every time they put their foot down in that race to a kill; dogs like Elka risk their lives every single time they run in pursuit of their prey.

I do, however, feel guilty about Angel's death. She was only six years old, and we'd gone to bash out a wood for some nuisance muntjac which were chomping their way through a plantation of young trees. The bigger wood stood alongside the plantation, and that day I'd taken Angel merely to slip her if something came out into the open, for she was soft-muscled at the time, enduring the post-season blubber to which most bitches succumb after a heat. Ligaments stretch and slacken, fat builds up round the heart, and the normally well-toned muscles 'break down' and soften, losing their strength. All this is due to the surge of hormones after a bitch's heat, a natural event as the body prepares for pups, whether or not the bitch has been mated.

I curse myself, even now, for slipping Angel on a muntjac as it sped in and out of the big trees, a diminutive barrel on legs, going like the clappers, like Road Runner; like a small, sharp tank on speed. Angel disappeared in its wake, and never came back. We searched the woods for half an hour before I finally heard a faint howl in the distance, and I eventually found my little blue bitch, lying still in the leaf matter, right up against the all too solid trunk of a tall tree. She had broken her back and was paralysed from the neck down, only able to lift her head slightly as she heard my approach. I knelt and knew the damage instantly; I'd seen it before. I soothed her with quiet words. The keeper was with us. He had a gun. Andy did the necessary as I stood in front of Angel, talking to her, telling her to look at me, away from her death.

I shouldn't have slipped her in that soft state, but who's to say that she wouldn't have met her maker even if she'd been fit and strong? Who's to say that the little blue bitch, who had lived so many days as a tiger amongst tigers, had finally run out of days, of lives? That her time had come? Nonetheless, I still feel responsible for her death, especially as I'd promised myself I'd only have slipped her if something came out into the open.

Do the events in our lives add up to a finite number? Is the script already written at the time of our birth, or even at the time of our conception? Is the journey already planned by some cosmic map maker? Does the number of days, the months and the years, all engraved in the stars, finally add up to some greater mathematical solution than we can ever know?

The deaths of some dogs hit harder than others. Angel was the end of that mini-line of wonderful fox dogs. I never bred from her, and I still get that knot of erupting sadness in the pit of my stomach when I think of the day she died. She should have gone on. She should have been with me for many years more. I've lost dogs at a younger age than her, but Angel was Angel. She was special, and sweet. Where her dam, Elka, lived truly on the 'dark side', Angel lived in the light, not a nasty bone in her body, everyone's friend and happy to just be alive, even when being alive was simply enjoying a nap in the sunshine alongside her canine pals. I still miss you Angel, and dammit, I'm sitting here writing this with tears in my eyes ... even all these years later.

Roe in a winter garden. Photo: Martin Prior.

~ An Honest Dog ~
by Joe

I had found myself dogless but it was not for the lack of trying as I had been scanning adverts in the field sports press for months, and even tried placing a wanted advert here and there. But eventually I had stumbled into purchasing a brindle puppy after a long phone call following an advert I had placed for a Deerhound, Greyhound Collie type, which was what I was set on at the time. The litter sounded very promising so I just had to have a look and travelled the several hundred miles a few days later. I say stumbled into it, as he was not bred the way I had asked in the advert at all! In fact he was out of a bitch called Elka who was the product of a mixed-bred lurcher to a Beardie Grey (Seeker) and the Sire (Merlin) was from a long line of lurchers, which had been doing the business for many years and they also had a pretty mixed ancestry. But all the dogs involved had something in common and that was they had all worked to a standard to be suitable to be bred from.

When I picked him he was a little larger than I had expected, which did give me some concerns, but his temperament really made my mind up as he was a very laid back and easy-going pup and he was obviously very well socialised. Another aspect I was set on was a rough-coated pup, which was something I had wanted; I know that colour or coat type doesn't matter, but I was fond of rough-coated dogs as I had grown up with them as a child. I did hope that he would turn rough or at least broken-coated due to his ancestry, but he never developed a coat like that, but instead produced a good dense short coat which was actually ideal. In short, I was travelling the long journey home to the shrill overtures of a whining pup of which if I am totally honest, didn't really resemble what I had set out to get. But never the less I was happy with him and as with any new pup I was filled with optimism for what the future held for the both of us.

He progressed well as a sapling and responded well to training. He self-entered to rabbit at just six months as he was lucky to have been of the right age to coincide with a bout of myxomatosis. This hideous disease only has one benefit in my world and that is supplying an opportunity for young dogs to catch, which really boosts that all important confidence that a young dog so needs. The hours of retrieve training paid off or maybe he just naturally had it in him but that first rabbit was brought back to hand like an old professional. His training went well, but as with all dogs it had its stressful moments which left me thinking 'is this dog ever going to make it' but those moments soon faded and he became a biddable dog and nice and easy to live with. His natural aptitude to hunt and just switch on always amazed me, and by the time he was 12 months old he had grown into a 26in, 28kg fast, racy animal. That speed was to be one of his biggest attributes during his hunting career.

It was around this age he self-entered to roe with quite some style, or maybe as I saw it then, a good dose of luck. It was autumn and we were on our usual early morning exercise across the fields, hunting along the hedges which culminated in a few futile runs on rabbits which were way too close to the hedge for the dog to be in with any sort of chance, but he had that optimism of youth which only a young dog has. We decided to enter a small field from a farm track which had a strip of rough ground on the left next to a hedge; the farmer had always left this area of the field alone most likely due to its camber, as I can remember it being this way all of my life. The strip consisted of tall grass and dieing brown bracken, with several large bramble patches.

The rest of the field was plough, and rose away to the right of us and at its furthest point in front of us it was bordered by a sparse excuse for a hedge. The other side of this hedge the next field dropped off very dramatically into one side of a very steep valley which was almost like a large natural amphitheatre. The dog had instantly scanned the plough as soon as we entered the field and as he cantered into the centre his head rose to draw in the scent just like one of the kids from the old Bisto adverts; then he was away left handed and entered the rough strip of ground. He worked down through the grass and bracken tight to the hedge and I could just keep an eye on where he was when he sprang up high. After a few seconds the pace soon picked up and the noise of crunching leaves and snapping twigs broke the silence.

With a crash three roe broke from the rough on to the plough and they were travelling; the two does who came out first peeled off right-handed, but the buck was last to leave the cover and he had the dog hot on his heels. They ran out from the cover on to the plough where the dog started to pressure the buck and forced his first turn which took them crashing back into the cover, and at this point I could see the dog actually stood a chance. I have found when a roe hits cover or comes across an obstacle under pressure, it will lose pace, and this is the time that a good experienced dog would have caught his deer.

The dog showed his inexperience or maybe he was just unlucky as this fella was flying and going by his antlers, was certainly no youngster; he sure knew where he was heading. The course continued the length of the cover and by now I was running to keep sight of them, and with another turn right-handed the buck headed back for the plough and then towards the sparse hedge at the end of the field with the dog laid on tight behind. Both dog and beast left the field through the hedge and were now out of sight and presumably going down the valley side, which was sure to be to the dog's disadvantage and most likely lead to a fruitless run.

My lungs were feeling the cold air now and I could not hear a thing while running, so I stopped for a second to see if I could catch any noise which would confirm he had caught, but I could not hear a thing. I was sure I was soon to see the dog coming back any minute with his tongue a foot long, but I continued to jog up the field. I went through the hedge and found myself at the top of the valley and no more than 50 yards below me was the dog, tail in the air, fast hold of his buck by the neck on one of the steepest parts of the valley! I was there quickly and did what needed to be done and the dog was soon rubbing his face in the dewy grass in celebration with what seemed to be a smile a mile wide. I can tell you he was not the only one smiling that autumn morning! Not only had he caught his first roe buck, he had managed it in a very difficult and awkward spot and he had chosen the correct hold and managed the situation well. From that morning on the dye had been cast; he had chosen his vocation in life, and no pre-empting situations from me were going to change that.

From that point on, his whole demeanour changed, he had grown up. There was less of the goofy puppy when in the fields just the more serious meaningful behaviour of an adult lurcher who had realised what he was bred for. From here on in I started working him on the lamp for rabbits and although not what I would term a fantastic rabbit dog due to his size and build he managed to consistently put a good few in the bag that first winter, which carried on for most of his life. He had a few faults, on rabbits he started to 'stand-off' on squatters instead of running in, and slowly started to pick his runs as he got older, especially if he considered they were too close to the hedge. Both faults used to irritate me no end as I am sure they would any keen lamper. However, he still took plenty of good hauls on the rabbits and a good number of hares, but when it came to roe he didn't disappoint.

Over the first season we had bumped into several roe simply while mooching for rabbits or out on exercise. I had noticed that a pattern was developing as a good percentage were taken in incredibly short distances which was quite simply due to his early pace and not being afraid to get hold of and tumble his quarry at the first given opportunity. Now don't get me wrong he was no super dog and it was clear to see he often relied on that early pace to get catches, but it did bring results.

At the time I was also coursing fairly regularly and had also ran him once on the fens where he did himself justice and caught two from three runs. He had typically caught his hares quickly and most were not the sort of long testing courses so suited to the saluki greyhound hybrid you see coursing on fenland. However, the fens were a totally different ball game to the ground I regularly coursed; the huge fields that seemed to be the size of a small county were quite simply unbelievably huge to me. The ground we were used to was flat beautiful peaty ground with dykes just like the Lincolnshire fens that was for sure, but it was like a miniature version. On this ground you needed an up-and-at-them dog who would move heaven and earth to get to terms with his hare before it was gone through a hedge or out of view. Luckily he was fairly well suited to this ground and we had some great courses over those few years, but the few he caught were down to his unsporting and slightly ungraceful technique of breakneck speed. A good example of this was an informal mid-week meet on some excellent running ground that usually held a good number of hares.

My friend and I had been 'drawn' together, his bitch was a well versed collie-bred animal and we had not coursed them together before so we were both looking forward to seeing a good tester for them ... if we were in luck. We had been 'drawn' higher in the numbers, so if we didn't see many hares it could be a lot of walking and maybe no chance to run our dogs. Unfortunately for us the day turned out to be quite slow and not many hares showed themselves to be suitable for a course and although we had seen several they rose just too far ahead. We did manage to view some good courses that morning and we were getting through the card slowly but time was getting on when we finally got into slips. Both dogs were to be in single slips and when we were given the word from the field marshal that the hare had enough law (50 yards) we were to slip together. We had chosen to do this rather than use the double slips which were for some reason unreliable.

The field was grass which was a few inches long with a few tussocks of reeds here and there. It had dykes on two sides, one behind us and a much larger one at the far end of the field, and reasonably thick hedges to our left and right hand sides. The plan was to walk this field to the end and then go through an old metal gate in the bottom left hand of the field and walk the adjoining field back up the opposite way. The line fanned out across most of the field without to many gaps and we moved off. We were nicely positioned in the middle of the line to be able to view most of the field ahead. My heartbeat upped a gear in anticipation as we set off, every movement of grass in the wind or snipe taking flight got the dog pulling stronger and my heart beating harder. We kept moving at a brisk pace down the field and as we reached just past the half-way point my optimism started to fade. As we now only had a few hundred yards of field to go. I had hoped we wouldn't raise a hare at the very bottom of the field to watch it lollop of into the distance for a 'no course'; not when we only had an hour to go at best to find another. But within a few yards up jumped 'Puss' heading left-handed, running parallel to the hedge about 20 yards out! Time stood still, just waiting to hear the words to let this crazy whining dog go as the hare made ground in the direction of the old gate in the corner of the field. Then the words "slip" rang out and the dogs were off.

Both dogs headed of towards Puss and the run up was pretty even between the dogs, they were making ground fast, but the hare knew where she was going and went over a rise close to the hedge. We could see the hare slip through the gate in the corner of the field from our elevated position. But the dogs had not seen this being lower to the ground and within a few yards my friend's dog went unsighted and put its nose down on the hunted hare's line. My dog had not slowed down at all, but was heading in a straight line for the end of the field! He was fast approaching the large dyke at the end of the field which he proceeded to jump, only just making the incline of the dyke on the other side. Then we realised what was happening and that a fresh hare had risen in the field the other side of the dyke at literally the same time as the hunted hare had gone through the gateway. This hare was up to speed and heading diagonally across the next field and she was trying her best to straightline my dog. The dog was now snapping at her heels and within a few hundred yards without a turn or a wrench the dog went down a gear and literally scooped it up on the move! If felt as though the people in the line fell quiet, and I am sure we were all thinking the same thing, that's not coursing that's catching!

It may have been totally unsporting to the dyed in the wool greyhound coursing folk but that to me was what a lurcher should be, an efficient catcher of game. As he negotiated the way back with his prize in his mouth, I met him at the dyke side with a proud smile. By the time he was into his second and third season I was working him very regularly, maybe a few night lampings a week and then some daytime work which could be mooching, or coursing when I could make a meet or had an invite. I am sure many will be able to relate when I say that every missed

Photo: 'Joe'

opportunity to work him was a shame. He thrived on the work load and was as fit as the proverbial flea. He sustained a few injuries in the line of duty but luckily nothing that a good rest or a chiropractor could not fix, which looking back on it was pretty amazing due to his style and speed.

But we have had our fair amount of close calls, in particular, the following sticks out in my mind, maybe it was skill or luck but I was glad of the outcome.

It was early morning and it looked as though the day would unfold into a fresh clear day. The plan was to have a quick walk out on a few fields I had permission on and maybe a run if we were lucky, then back home for breakfast, more than likely before half the population's alarm clocks had even gone off. This is one of my favourite times of day, as we arrived on the land there was light dew on the ground and a few patches of mist lying in the hollows and woodland that we had to walk through. The fields we were heading to had been planted with winter wheat and they all sloped away to our left downhill. The two main fields were divided by a thin hedge which had a few trees in sporadic patches along its length and at the highest point to our right was a large double hedge with some thick cover full of oaks and ash trees. I planned to walk along the double hedge and then walk left handed down the fields towards the thin hedge to see what was there. The idea being if we saw any roe, which were most likely to be in the double hedge, that we would push them off and hope to bump into a hare for a run.

I had the dog on a slip and as we were about to enter the first field tight to the double hedge we noticed Reynard ambling towards us totally unaware of our presence; we watched for a few minutes till he saw us, and with his brush held high he leapt back into the double hedge and was gone. We proceeded along the hedge line, scanning the field before us; the dog was pulling on the slip and my heart upped a gear just waiting for that sudden burst of adrenalin of when a hare rises. We walked the full length of the hedge until we met the adjoining hedge without a thing happening and no roe to push off as I had planned. I had started to curse Reynard for ruining our sport. Well, we still had a field to go, so we walked down hill and before we hit the next hedge puss rose up 20 yards out! The slip fell to my side, and my hound was away, he was close to his quarry straight away and rightly so, this was no place to be giving a hare fair law if you wanted to catch one. They both headed up the field back towards the double hedge and the dog boxed her off nicely when they went out of sight. I was on my toes and running to the highest point to get a view. I saw the dog was still up close and personal and they were now in the centre of the field doing a few circles; you could see he had the hare rattled and it looked to be going his way. But just as it looked like he had it in the bag she made a break for it and made ground on the dog from a tight turn and straight lined him to a hedge which they both went through like butter, but the dog was trailing. Again they had gone out of view and I ran to the hedge to see if I could see them again, but it was useless. I waited a while getting my breath back from my lap of the field and hoped the dog would be back with his prize as he had worked hard. But sadly before long there was a rustle in the hedge and there he was with a tongue a foot long and his sides heaving.

100

Well, after doing laps of the field and the dog needing to get his tongue in I left him off the slip to relax for a minute or two, but he didn't get 30 seconds! Directly behind us two roe broke from one of the small clusters of trees from the dividing hedge … they must have been there the whole time laid down! The dog didn't waste any time and picked his doe and started making ground as they went away up the hill. He put some pressure on and turned it from its course which swung it right-handed down towards the double hedge. I ran up the field to try and keep them in view, they were up to speed now and I was willing him to pull it and end things, but he just couldn't quite get there. Both of them were running the edge of the trees now at close terms, the dog put in a strike and with a dull thud the doe hit a tree within a few inches of the dog and both of them cartwheeled into a heap. The dog was straight up and took hold but she was not moving. She had hit that tree at such speed she was dead instantly. I have seen many roe taken in trees and at the edge of woods, as they often slow down when approaching cover, but I'd not seen a head-on collision with a tree before. It could just as easily have been the dog lying there instead of the deer. I can remember as I walked back to the car with the roe over my shoulder thinking of the 'what ifs' but luck had shone on us that morning and the breakfast of fresh roe liver on toast was welcomed by us both.

Without trying to sound too clichéd I feel that luck had played its part in both mine and the dog's life. He served me for many seasons but as with many things in life his luck eventually ran out when he suffered an accident which left me with that one last tough decision. He suited my life at the time as there were no regulations to limit what we could and couldn't do. That pup from the wrong breeding which I stumbled into buying all those years ago ended up leading me on quite some adventures. He turned into an honest dog which took the full gamut of quarry and I consider myself lucky to have owned him. I don't think you can ask for more than that.

~ Hare dogs ~

Why does the hare fascinate me so? What is it about this relatively small animal that has so much power to excite and enthral? To the uninitiated, the hare is quite insignificant when compared to a large wild animal such as a deer. To those who know nothing of the hare's athletic ability, it is merely a larger rabbit, one which lives in the open, exposed to all weather, finding no refuge in burrow or den.

~ THOUGHTS ON THE HUNT FOR THE HARE ~

Get up close to a hare, if you can, and you'll see something totally different to the rabbit. With its startled gold eyes, longer ears and a permanently slightly tousled air of one roused from the depths of deep sleep, the hare incites in the hunter an emotion of greedy desire. Hares do not look cute or cuddly, unless they are only a few weeks of age; their expression is that of a haunted, wild spirit, a creature of myth and mystery.

The perfectly camouflaged hare, with its coat flecked in hues of sand, cream and brown, lies motionless in its seat. You think you see a hare from a distance, but once you walk towards it, it seems to vanish, as if by magic, into the smallest patch of cover, pressing its body close to the blending colours of grass or leaves.

I have often walked strips of old pheasant cover down the edges of fields in mid-winter, when grass and weeds are brown and sparse. I have walked within inches of hares, never knowing their presence unless some chance instinct has made me look down, and as you catch that wide, staring eye with your own, the hare leaps from its place of hiding, knowing that its cover is blown. And although you attempt to follow its flight through the dead grasses of winter, once the hare is more than 60 or 70 metres away, it is almost impossible to keep the fleeing form in sight, such is its ability to blend with its surroundings. Only on the open fields can you keep your eyes trained on that little brown shape as it races away in the distance.

To the experienced eye, it is possible to discern the double hump of the hare's head and rump as it lies in the field, though deep, furrowed plough can make this impossible. Even on short winter wheat the hare can appear to squash its body into the ground, vanishing from view. Of course, this also depends on whether the hare is actually lying in a form (seat) or merely atop the ground.

There's a saying which goes: 'on seeing a lump in a field, if it gets smaller it's a hare, if not, it's a stone'. And how true that is! But not always! We saw one such 'brick' once. A rectangular shape, for all the world like a house brick lying in a field. We drove past, thinking that a hare would have got down, altered shape. Half an hour later, as we returned along the fen drove, the 'brick' was still there, and Andy's young son insisted that it was indeed a hare.

He was right. I walked out to it and before I could get within a hundred yards of the 'brick', it had jumped. I slipped my dog, which was then taken on a punishing run across the fen. That was a confident hare indeed, and it escaped unscathed. The mystery of the supposedly rectangular shape of the 'brick' was of course due to the low winter sun as it created sharp lines of light and shade on the living creature.

And then there's the supreme athletic ability of the hare. Few other creatures of similar size are able to maintain top speed for so long without pausing to rest. No other wild animal has the ability to twist, turn and jink like the hare (though a fox on the lamp comes pretty close) and few creatures incite such peaks of emotion, such a desperate need for possession. The brown hare is the supreme target for running dogs, and only dogs of similar ability to the hare will catch them on a regular basis.

The pursuit of the hare with dogs is one of the oldest forms of sport or hunting in the world. The ancient Egyptians used sighthounds to hunt and catch hares, and the sport has continued ever since. Actually, I don't like the term 'sport', as it demeans the whole concept in my eyes. A sport is something you do for fun, a way to pass time when not at work. Hunting with dogs, hare coursing in particular, is so much more than any sport could ever be. It's a passion that fires the blood of both hound and human.

Don't get me wrong, I'm not demeaning rabbits in the slightest, and they're not the easiest thing to catch either, running for home on ground they know like the back of their paw. It's just that hares have a different mystique about them altogether.

~ MINA ~

I have not always kept specialist lurchers during my life; I'm too much of a pot hunter, an opportunistic creature who needs dogs of the same ilk, but I have been fortunate enough to own one or

Mina.

two decent hare dogs. For 15 years I was secretary of, and ran dogs with the East of England Lurcher Club on the flat lands of Lincolnshire. Mina was the first specialist hare dog I owned, and the first real coursing-bred bitch compared to the others who could turn their paws to other forms of work with just as much skill and ability. I found Mina at a lurcher show. Who in their right minds would seriously look at puppies for sale at a show? A lottery if ever there was one. No more chance of finding a good 'un than if you stuck your hand into a lucky dip to come out with a worthwhile prize.

There were nine pups (they were nine weeks of age) on leads and little collars, scrambling, tangling and playing in the sun, unfazed by the crowds and numerous dogs all around. Brindles and reds, their coats shone with health, and I looked and looked, and eventually my eye was taken with one bright brindle pup, which, frustrated by the restriction of the lead, had taken to digging up the turf and was throwing morsels of earth and roots into the air, catching them as they fell back to the ground.

Leverets sunning themselves after a summer rain storm ...

Almost hidden.

I walked away, but I couldn't stop thinking about that pup. A few days later I saw the advert in the *Countryman's Weekly*. I phoned, I described the pup I'd liked, and I travelled to the Midlands to meet up with the breeder. They were well-bred, so I was told, but the breeder was a relative novice to the game, and I had only his word as to the working ability of the parents. I took the pup home, and so began my life with Mina.

She was bonkers. She was over-sensitive in the way that only Saluki lurchers can be, and she was also comical, charming and as dainty as a ballet dancer. All knobbly bones, stick thin legs and floppy ears, with those almond-shaped eyes that gave her a slightly alien look: a far cry from those pedestrian, base-blooded lurchers that I'd kept until then. Mina was easily spooked, easily offended and prone to flights of fancy: black bin bags by the side of the road were lurking monsters waiting to devour passers-by; hot air balloons were aliens in the skies above and she danced like a cat as she swatted at birds in the garden.

She never saw hares as a pup, and she didn't have the early pace needed to snatch up the rabbits which were running for home, though I'm sure that she managed to snaffle-up the occasional, unwary young bunny. If I remember rightly, she saw her first hare at around 14 months of age, at a doubled-up meeting, and straight away she knew, through instinct and those inherited genes, just what to do. This was what she had been born for. I remember Don Southard saying to me, several weeks after that first hare, that he'd never seen a dog 'learn' hares as fast as Mina; she understood how to run them almost immediately.

Mina was a good hare dog, maybe not the best, but good all the same. Her lungs and heart were naturally strong from a puppy-hood spent running for fun, but even the long, sleek muscles of a Saluki-saturated lurcher need miles of bike work and steady trotting to tighten those sinews and tendons, to imbue those muscles with the strength they need to compete with a hare which might run for miles at top speed every day of its life.

Mina's hares were not kick-ups either. Each hare she ran was afforded fair law in the club. This means 100 metres or more, especially when doubled up (running under NCC rules). When running single-handed you had to slip at 50 metres or more and woe betide the person who short-slipped. The run wouldn't count if you'd been seen to slip short, no matter how long the course went on, and whether or not the dog actually caught or not. Tough rules indeed.

A dog needed speed as well as stamina to run under those conditions. The energy expended just getting to the hare, already up and running flat out the moment it jumped, was enormous. Those hares knew exactly what dogs could do. They were run, both by poachers and legitimate coursers, all winter long, even in the summer they weren't safe. The moment the corn had been cut, the poachers would drive on to the land, slipping on kick-ups and boasting that their dogs could do three out of three, four out of four.

A half-grown leveret shouldn't pose much problem for even a very average dog, but a three-quarter grown hare can twist and turn very well. Thankfully many of the poachers must have been running less than average dogs, for despite the annual slaughter of young hares the moment the corn had been cut, there were usually plenty of fit, strong beasts left on the fens come autumn. By the time we started running, in late October, the weak had gone and come January, none but the super fit, the clever and the strong remained, and they had tricks up their sleeves which left inexperienced or sub-standard dogs wallowing in their wake. Some had also learned to go to ground, flying into drains and rabbit holes under pressure. Oh no, these weren't easy, green hares at all.

The following are accounts of three runs which stand out in my mind; all but one were run in competition. I can't remember in what order they were run, but I do remember that on one particular day, Mina was the only dog to catch on the land in question. But I'll start with a run on the hills. This wasn't flat land at all. We'd been invited up into the hills of the Lincolnshire wolds, a group of us. It was a cold winter's day, and I surveyed the rising land with amazement, having been used to running on the fens where you could see for miles in every direction.

~ THE HARE ON THE HILL ~

There were good dogs out that day, experienced dogs which could read a hare well, and all around us were small spinneys, places of safety for hard-pressed hares. I wish I could remember the other dogs which were out that day, but many years have passed; not only does our subjective human mind prefer to retain the details of our own dogs, but I never carried a camera in those days, without which the details become hazy and blurred. I can only remember the one run of Mina's though I do know that she caught two hares that day.

Andy was slipping Mina as I think that I'd brought two dogs, the other a little bitch who sometimes ran well, and at other times jacked for no apparent reason. More of her later, as she became dam to another good bitch of mine.

We were walking up an endless hill; the field must have been nearly a mile in length, rising steeply all the time. To our right lay a road, to our left a deeply indented valley, which led up to a small open spinney of straggly trees. The field was rape, but stunted and low, bar one block or around 200 square metres which had grown to a height of around 18 inches.

A hare jumped far ahead, we were struggling for hares at the time. It was well over 100 metres away, maybe more, and Mina had seen the hare jump; Andy slipped her, and I cursed him for sending the dog off on an impossible mission. This wasn't flat land where a dog could keep its target in sight no matter how long the slip. Just as I expected it to do, the hare, on reaching the taller stand of rape, executed a sharp left turn and vanished from sight, down towards the valley.

Mina ran straight to the spot where she'd last seen the hare, and she bounced. She leapt into the air like a kangaroo, looking first to the right as she reached the highest point of her bounce: nothing there, and then bounced again, looking this time to the left, and she must have spied her target, though we could see nothing of the fleeing animal. She set off again, vanishing behind the increasingly tall rape plants.

Then nothing, until one of our party let out a shout: "There she is!" and I spotted the dog in the wood, down in the valley, a brindle shape nipping in and out of the straggly trees. She was bounding over the fallen branches, twisting and turning in and out of the bare winter wood, and there was the hare, several yards before her, running for its life.

Had there been undergrowth still fresh and green in that wood, Mina would have no doubt lost her hare immediately it penetrated that place of refuge, but this was deep winter, and only bare bramble stems caught at her legs as she tried to follow the hare.

Out of the wood they came, but the bitch was too close and the hare turned back in a frantic attempt to lose her between the trees once more. Its tactic was pointless, for so long as the dog could see the small brown form in front of her, she'd never stop, no matter what objects stood in her way.

Out of the wood once more, I could see that the hare was beginning to panic. The dog saw it too, and for what seemed an eternity, she danced the dance of death round that hare. The hare span and twisted in ever decreasing circles, with the bitch breathing hard on its back, and Neil, at my shoulder, said "Go ON! Pick it UP!" For although Mina's strike was usually decent, she didn't seem able to finish this course. She'd been running on a hillside, and her legs were not used to the punishing rise of the land. Later I'd find that she'd bruised her chest badly as she'd crashed through the wood, over branches and fallen trees.

Finally, the bitch stooped her head and lifted the hare. Neil said, "Surely you're not going to make her retrieve it after a run like that!" I walked towards Mina, who was struggling to carry the hare back to me. She always retrieved, not matter what distance had to be covered, but between us now lay a deep gulley in the valley bottom and she was hesitating on the side of the drop, trying to gather up the necessary energy to make the leap.

I ran down the hill and dropped into the gulley and hauled myself up the other side, praising the bitch mightily. Her eyes shone in recognition of my praise, and her tail beat slowly from side to side. These were the best of times, when she brought her hares back after a long run. She'd come in like an old gundog, head held high, no matter how exhausted she was, wagging her tail just like a Labrador. She loved the success, she loved the praise, and she only ever put the hare down when my hand was reaching out for it. Safe at last.

~ BETWEEN THE SEA WALL BANKS ~

Lightly-built lurchers can run on any type of ground, even fields which are saturated swamps, fields which sap the energy from most dogs and especially those which aren't quite fit enough or are more heavily built. Mina could run on wet, deep land because she floated, her running style was, on the run up, almost Whippety. Her back bowed and straightened like that of a cheetah as she raced to get on terms with her quarry, but once she reached it she flattened out and blew across the open ground like a feather, effortlessly linked to her prey by an invisible thread of force and desire. She knew how to adjust her running style to the ground on the day, and she knew when to surge forwards and when to hold back.

Only 45lbs in weight fully fit, but measuring dead on 25 inches to the shoulder, Mina could run on ground that left most dogs floundering. On the day in question, she would need every ounce of willpower and strength she possessed in order to catch her hare.

We were walking between the two sea walls on the coast in Lincolnshire, as far as you can go to the east of England without falling into the sea. The old sea wall is a low grassy bank, settled down over the years to a height of no more than ten feet or so. It is speckled with hawthorn bushes and long grass in places where sheep have not grazed it smooth, and inland lie miles upon miles of fertile arable land, reclaimed from the sea when first the salt marshes were drained during the 17th century by methods which were refined by the Dutchman Vermuyden, an expert at making the flat salt marshes into a rich arable resource. They'd had a lot of practice in Holland.

To the east, on the coast side of the old sea wall, lies more recently reclaimed land; the soil is deep, a fine sediment that clutches at your boots as you walk, but falls freely as you lift your foot again. A dog, when running hard, sinks deeply at every step, the smaller surface area of its feet offering less resistance to its weight. Hares barely dent the surface of the ground: they are light and their feet touch down but briefly as they run.

The distance between the sea walls is about half a mile; half a mile of perfectly flat land, and then the 'new' bank rises from the end of the field. This newer bank is high, higher than a two-storey house, and its sides are as steep as a house roof. It is covered in long, thick dry grass, and livestock graze it during the summer months.

But there's wire, fences of the stuff every few hundred yards, winding its way up the side of the bank, and forming a barrier into the arable fields at its base. Beyond the bank lie the salt marshes, where samphyre and marsh grass grow. The grey mud is laced with a thousand small creeks where unwary wildfowlers have sometimes been drowned in their desire to shoot just one more bird as the tide came in. Further still to the east lies the sea, visible only as a long dark strip against the horizon. It is a wild and inhospitable place and it fills me with a yearning to stay there forever when I look out at the barren reaches, towards that line where the land meets the sea.

But I'm not on the bank now, I'm walking the field, and we're midway between the two sea-wall banks; once again Andy is slipping. I'm not a good slipper. I tend to be a bit trigger happy! Slipping too soon, forgetting the fair law our club has imposed, it's easier for me to let Andy slip. He has a cool head and has slipped for the club for many seasons now, though some of his slips leave me raging inside: so far! How can any dog even get to the hare before it hits cover!

Andy knows Mina's capabilities as well as I do, and he's slipped her on a long swinging hare which is belting towards the old sea-wall bank. Even so, I really do wonder if this time he has misjudged the distance, leaving the dog no time to turn the hare from the safety of the bank. The hare is rapidly closing the distance to the grassy rise in the distance, and Mina is still over 70 metres behind it. But she gets there, flying over the soft ground like an over-sized Whippet, back arching and bowing, muscles bunching and straining as she gallops furiously, determined not to let it leave the field.

She's made it! She's run round the hare and forced it away from the bank, and I see her relax a little, see her head come up, watching, reading her quarry's intentions, but the hare puts on a spurt, gains some ground, and darts back to the right, to the bank, and Mina finds gears, punishing her body as she runs a tight curve on that spongy, silty ground, and she's swooping in from the left to force her target into a sharp turn, back to the open field again.

Time and again I see the bitch accelerate, and time and again I see the hare flatten its ears and drop down a gear to compcte with the onslaught from behind. Six, seven, eight times or more, the duel continues until the hare gives up on its mission to make for the bank. It turns out to the open field, foiled for the moment, and heads in the opposite direction, for the far bank, nearly half a mile away. And Mina follows her target, head up, panting hard now. She's won the first round, and she lets the hare run, knowing that the creature is far too strong to be killed just yet.

I'm vaguely aware of Gary Dickinson standing next to me; he's been talking quietly, watching the dog, analysing her moves "Head down, going in, head up, letting it run, leaving it ..." Such are the trivial things you remember when watching a great run; things of no real consequence, but important as part of the memory as a whole.

Down the field they come, right past me, and I hear the slap of her feet on the wet soil and see her eyes fixed hard on the hare as it runs. Its ears are half-cocked now, and it's no longer panicking, though it's racing flat out with the bitch just

113

a metre or so behind it. Mina flows after the hare, watching it, waiting, running easily like a marathon runner, matching her quarry for pace, but taking that all-important breather. She too knows the challenge that rises before her, the fast approaching shape of the high bank. They reach the edge of the field, and the hare flits through the strands of barbed wire like a wisp of brown smoke, across the dyke beyond, and it races up the side of the bank, barely visible amongst the dried strands of grass.

Mina follows, but she's lost ground negotiating the fence, and the hare has 20 metres on her now. Both dog and hare disappear over the brow of the bank, and my eyes sweep desperately back and forth along the length of my horizon. Pursued and pursuer are back in sight, racing up and down the bank. The climbs are punishing to the dog, only slightly less so to the hare, its long hind legs able to handle the incline with less problem. But it is beginning to tire, and the bitch is still there, ploughing determinedly in its wake. I can see her exhaustion too; her legs move woodenly, her movement almost mechanical.

This has become a battle of attrition. Who will win? Who will succeed? Life against death. Is the dog's need to kill greater than the hare's will to live? Or is the hare strong enough to hold on to its life in the face of death?

The answer comes swiftly as the hare breaks back for the field once more, having failed to lose the predator in the long grass of the bank, but the bitch is too close, and she lunges forward, tumbling over and over with her prey at the bottom of the bank. That tiny hesitation, the hare's split-second indecision as it chose its route, not really wanting the open field with half a mile of ground to cover before reaching the second bank in the distance; that microsecond in time sealed its fate.

It's over. I run to her, not wanting her to even attempt a retrieve after such a run. I've lived each beat of her heart as she ran, felt the pain in my muscles as in hers, and as I gasp lungfuls of air at the end, only then do I notice that I'd been almost holding my breath while she ran, breathing shallow and fast all the time I'd been watching the course.

Of course Mina didn't catch every hare she ran, and one day she failed on the very same ground, on the same bank. The hare had taken her up on to the new sea wall bank, then back out on to the field once more. It had run round a dew pond, and finding the bitch still grimly hanging on only a couple of metres behind, had come straight back through the line of spectators and dogs and flashed to ground in a hole, the end of a land drain in a small dyke that bisected the field. So close behind the hare was Mina that she'd grabbed fur from its rear as it entered the hole. Pale tufts of hair scattered the entrance and blew away on the breeze as I approached, and as I looked into the darkness I could make out the rump of the hare as it sat bunched in terror, but safe. I could have pulled it out with my hand! But I didn't, though I do remember a certain person exclaiming, at the time, from his position on the top of the bank, that I was pulling the hare out of the hole in an attempt to claim the course unsportingly! That person shall remain nameless, and I wonder if he mistook my intentions, which were merely of wanting to see the hare, to verify its existence in that place. I needed to see it lying tight in its refuge; to know it was there and that the animal hadn't just vanished into thin air! Not a sneaky attempt to lay physical claim to the beast. People often read into the deeds and thoughts of others what they might do or think themselves! And competition coursing brings out the worst in humans, which is one reason I've never matched for money.

I've got the wrong temperament for such games, and I'll freely admit that whilst winning a course or a competition became almost a holy grail for me, I'd never have stooped to the cheating methods that others have used. I might have hated to lose, but I'd sooner lose a course or a hare than my self-respect. I love coursing because it is the ultimate contest between predator and prey. On the one hand you have a creature of almost supernatural ability, a creature that has evolved, over time, to become the strongest and fastest of its kind.

And then you have the dog, the specialist, the marathon runner; an animal which has evolved through man's desire to create a beast of equal ability to that of the hare. Forget temperament, forget kennel club looks, and forget colour and type of coat. The only thing that matters when pursuing the dream of breeding a hare-catching hound is the performance.

Just as wild canines have evolved to a certain type and shape, so has the shape and ability of the hare dogs been defined by their function. Form follows function: of course it does, or it should, though to look at some of the man-made monstrosities within the canine world today, you have to ask yourself if the horrific nightmares of a madman were responsible for some of the deformities we see in the show ring.

That is the wonder and beauty of working dogs. Never have they had to satisfy a falsely-created criteria of physical beauty;

116

their beauty is in what they do, how they work, how they run. And of course they are beautiful! These canine athletes are more beautiful in every way than their distant relatives who mince along carpets under floodlit gatherings which gasp and say, "How perfect", when seeing a ridiculously extended trot from an animal which should have been formed for galloping.

Many of those high-stepping, unfit caricatures of dogs would struggle to run and catch hares. Although they may 'fit' a man-made blueprint of a hound built to run, their beauty can never compare with the genuine, bred-for-work dog.

Where hares have been coursed by dogs for generations, it is logical to suppose that only the fastest, the cleverest, and the strongest remain to breed from. Course these hares on a regular basis, and those without wit, speed or strength, must fall to the dogs. Thus does the strength and the quality of these hares continue to improve. This is natural selection in its most brutal form, and although it is us, we humans, who have prompted this evolution, through our desire to catch the hare, we are no different to the truly wild predators which have evolved to hunt and kill their prey. The only difference is that we've manipulated the genes of a fellow predator in order to succeed, rather than developing a body to do it ourselves!

We used to run on one farm, which was also a good rabbit place. The dyke sides on some fields were peppered with rabbit holes. When we first coursed this land the hares didn't go to ground, but over time, many seasons and years, they took to flitting down holes almost as readily as the rightful occupants of those warrens. People would groan in despair if their dogs were slipped on certain parts of this farm, for they knew that the hare would most likely make straight for the nearest warren, or land drain.

Land drains too made excellent refuges for the hares, and also the short drains beneath the 'bridges' between the fields. In the absence of hedges and gates, the dykes and drains were, in places, filled in to the width of a tractor, a concrete pipe being laid in the dyke bottom to allow drainage. Many is the time I've seen hares speed into these drains with a dog on their tail, leaving the bemused hound peering, frustrated, into the hole, while the quarry sped straight out of the other end and away to safety.

Of course this tactic only worked with relatively inexperienced dogs; seasoned lurchers who knew the land well, would have learned that such drains were a 'through route', and on seeing the hare vanish into the pipe, they'd leap up on to the field again, ready and waiting as the hare came out of the far end of the pipe, and the race would be on once more.

~ A HARE ON THE BLACK LAND ~

I was fortunate enough to have permission on some black land. This black land, as it is known in coursing circles, is rich and peaty. Arable farming began when the fens, which were vast areas of water and marsh stretching across parts of East Anglia, were drained in the 1600s. As the marshes dried out, bisected by great drains and dykes, the land shrank, and many places today are below sea level.

Like a sponge, this black land absorbs and retains moisture, and whilst it might be a joy to run on when dry, it draws a dog down when it's sodden with rain. It saps the strength of all dogs, heavy or light of build, though a featherweight runner is better off when the ground resembles an uncooked chocolate cake mix. Even the hares don't like to run on this ground at its wettest, as we'll see in this next account of a day on the Cambridgeshire fens.

If I remember rightly, we were on the first round of our single-handed competition. Mina should have been in her prime, at around three years of age, and I'd been granted access to a farm where the hares were not normally coursed, or so I thought. This was black land at its finest, hundreds of acres of prime dark peat, and not a stone in sight to gash the unwary pads of a dog.

I'd been drawn against a good, honest dog, but on paper he shouldn't have taken much beating. Blue was a trier, but he was running with only half his vision, having lost an eye through infection after a thorn had impaled the orb the previous season. He was a decent dog, but one who ran on guts and grim determination rather than outstanding natural ability; Mina, at the top of her game, should have beaten him easily, but when pitting one animal against another, the results can be surprising at times. It's a game of chance and luck; lots of luck. All we can do is to get our dogs fit for the occasion, well-fed and honed for the task before them.

Three runs each, that's all we needed, and I was quietly confident. You know the saying of course: pride goes before a fall! Well, we almost fell that day.

Mina was three weeks out of season, and I knew that she'd soon be approaching the period of soft-muscled, lax-limbed weakness to which many bitches are prone. It's all down to the hormonal changes which occur after a bitch's heat. Whether or not a bitch is truly in whelp, her body prepares for the eventuality of a litter. I thought Mina was still strong, that she wasn't yet suffering the effects of that annoying female cycle, so I'd not pulled her out of the competition.

On that late November morning, Mina caught her first hare easily, on a field of old stubble, but the second jumped on a disgusting slippery field where they'd just harvested sugar beet. The resulting mess of mud and smashed beet leaves made walking a nightmare. On the far side of the field lay the farm yard: several buildings and bits of machinery dotted about. I should never have slipped in this place, but I was too cocky, too sure of my bitch's ability.

I slipped Mina on a sideways-swinging hare, and the canny beast promptly made straight for the yard, with Mina slipping and sliding in its wake. Round the side of the first building she went, and I heard a cacophony of barking. Two farm Labradors came into sight, chasing my dog, which, never the bravest in the face of canine opposition, fled back to me as fast as her legs could carry her.

But she'd turned the hare once, and under the rules of the club, it had to count as a course. If this happened today I'd have argued against this rule, but no matter, those days are long gone now and it's all water under the bridge.

Mina's second hare jumped in the middle of a field of plough, and it made straight for the only tree to be seen for miles, right on the side of a dyke. Mina followed the hare across the dyke, turned it hard twice and then stopped dead by the tree: the hare had made it to ground in a hole at its base. Not good!

I was beginning to wonder just how naïve these hares actually were: so far they'd known very well where to run in times of need. I hadn't thought at the time that the farmer's Labradors were probably exercising the hares on a daily basis! And of course there were poachers; always there were poachers. I found out later from the farmer, who didn't normally allow coursing on his land, that he'd been increasingly plagued by gangs of poachers.

I can't remember Blue's first two runs, apart from the fact that he caught the second, which meant we were on level pegging at this stage. Blue's third hare led him around the same field of plough, and he was breathing down its neck for the whole run. I'm ashamed to think that I watched the dog run with a sinking feeling, knowing in my heart of hearts that any moment I'd have to walk over to Roger, and offer my hand in congratulation. That I'd have to accept the outcome in a sporting manner, and smile bravely, going home with the certain knowledge that fate hadn't been on my side that day.

But Blue failed to catch that hare. Darting and dodging the dog at every stride, it made the eventual safety of the river bank, over 200 metres away, where fallen trees and brambles hid its path the moment it left the field.

We still had everything to run for!

We entered a lower lying field of set-aside, where water lay visible in the long ruts between the rotting stems of vegetation. Surely too damp for a hare to sit snugly - I was wrong. Mina's hare jumped from among the sodden stems of old wheat, and splashed straight towards the drove. Droves are fen farm tracks, built up many years ago to carry horse and cart or plough between the bottomless fen fields. Most have been reinforced with rubble over the years, though some are grassed. The fens are a patchwork of droves, dykes and fields, and without the dykes there would be no fields: the whole area would be marshland.

Hares often choose to run along the droves, getting up real speed on the firmer ground before attempting to strike out across a field, often heading for a clump of trees or a land drain in the distance, once they think themselves far enough from the dog.

That is exactly what this hare did. It belted down the drove, kicking up spray in its wake, before turning sharply and heading out across a field which looked as though it could have been covered in black sludge. The hare was obviously heading for the river bank on the far side of the field, where a few sparse brambles and trees might offer some refuge.

Mina, about twenty metres behind the hare at this stage, followed her quarry out on to the black, oozing ground. And all of a sudden, it was as if someone had pressed the slow motion button on a film. From full speed to half throttle in a second, the dog ploughed, literally, through the earth; a thick, peaty morass which made galloping damn near impossible.

The hare was now about 50 metres in front of the dog, and it too was struggling to run as it should. Both animals were around 150 metres distant by now, and I shaded my eyes in an effort to distinguish the smaller form of the hare as it paddled desperately against the sucking ooze which threatened to drag it down. I tried to follow them on to the field, but the moment I set foot on that black, waterlogged soil I sank, almost up to my knees! I had to turn back and fast, trying to cover the ground in a shambling, bent legged shuffle; attempting to lift each foot quickly before I became set in the mud. I watched from the safety of the firm ground on the drove.

Was the dog gaining slightly? I couldn't be sure, but then the hare did something quite unexpected ... it turned, of its own volition, sweeping wide past the dog and headed back to the drove and firmer land. Had it thought there was no chance of making that distance across the field in safety? One thing's for sure, the dog never forced that hare to turn.

And Mina followed her target back across the black mud. Once back on firmer footing, she flattened out in a dead run, making a desperate attempt to close the gap between her and her prey. I didn't see the whole course, for the drove turned sharply at the end of the field, and both dog and hare vanished from sight for a second or two. When they came back into view, Mina was hard on the heels of her prey. As I strained my eyes to see detail at a distance of well over 200 metres, I could see both hare and dog come down the side of a grassy bank at the edge of the field. I saw the dog plunge the last few feet in a strike which brought her crashing head over heels, to finally claim her reward.

She started to retrieve that hare, but exhaustion got the better of her and she laid the hare down on the track, going straight to a large puddle of water to drink. This was one of only two times that she didn't retrieve the whole way back to me, and the first time I'd seen her go to water to assuage her thirst straight after a course. This bitch seldom drank anything at all, and if I wanted to get electrolytes into her after a gruelling run, I had to

A creature of myth and mystery.

do so fast, for she'd refuse to drink anything once she'd stopped panting.

We run our dogs on many types of ground, but it is only by walking that land, and understanding how conditions affect both dog and prey, that we can truly appreciate the unbelievable efforts they make, the one to kill, the other to survive.

~ ISHTAR ~

Named after the Indian goddess, daughter of the sun and the moon. Ishtar's dam was Lunar (the moon) and her sire was Solar (the sun). Both could catch hares with ease, and Solar had come from a long and illustrious line of coursing lurchers: Merlin, Eve, The Hoover, Del Tomlin's Luke to name but a few of those good ancestors.

Solar was small, only 23 inches and a tougher little dog I've never had. His drive was through the roof, and he killed himself running rabbits on my local landfill site, breaking his neck among the narrow gullies formed by the rain on the hill. He was only two and a half years of age, but had proved himself over and over again on all quarry.

Lunar was lurcher to lurcher too, but from a little rough bitch of breeding unknown put to a Saluki Greyhound. She was lightening fast, and quirky as hell. One day she'd pull out all the stops to catch a seemingly impossible hare, and the next, she'd jack on what appeared to be a sure thing. Not a bitch you'd want to gamble on if gambling was your thing.

I'll never forget seeing Lunar pull up on two hares one morning, hares which weren't 20 metres in front of her. Yet, in the afternoon, she ran on the boggiest, soggiest, most bottomless field you can imagine, and drove her hare to a virtual standstill in a marathon run, finally killing it in a dyke bottom. As I said, she was quirky as hell, though the two hares she'd jacked on in the morning had been fast nearing cover: sometimes a dog can be too imaginative for its own good!

Ishtar inherited the best bits from both her parents. She was fast, tough and she didn't jack, though she was slightly strange in some ways. Nervy, highly strung, but a joy to handle in the field.

Her first hare was killed at the age of nine months, and she left it in the hedge, running back to me as fast as her legs would carry her, worried to have found herself alone in a strange field. I put her into the club single-handed competition her first year of running, and she never retrieved a hare until the day of the final, after that she always retrieved her hares perfectly. There's nowt as strange as dogs!

Ishtar wasn't destined to make old bones either, and like her sire, died of a broken back after failing to leap the yawning abyss of a massive drain on the fens. I still find it hard to think of that day, which came at the end of a season's running where she barely put a foot wrong.

She was exciting to watch, all guts and gumption and wild speed. Small, at just under 23 inches, she could turn almost as tightly as a hare, and once she had it in her sights on drilling, you knew that its days were numbered. Funnily enough, and just like a hare, she found it harder to run over plough.

Where most dogs sail over plough with relative ease, Ishtar's rapid, pumping style of running combined with her small size, led her to trip and stumble just as hares do over rough ground. I can't count the number of times I saw Ish and hare fumbling over the plough, legs going all ways, the hare just keeping ahead of the dog, with neither making the sort of progress it should. Once on the wheat though, the hare was usually doomed. With Whippet speed, together with almost Saluki stamina, Ishtar burned her hares into the ground, turning them inside out within seconds, and finishing the run with a devastating strike.

I say 'almost' Saluki stamina, for the bitch wasn't a true marathon runner. Four minutes was her limit, though I've seen her hang on for five, and be absolutely exhausted afterwards, and with no surprise. No dog can run for that length of time at such a grindingly fast pace without burning itself into the ground. It seldom mattered, for most of her hares were killed in well under two minutes. I remember a day when she killed three out of four, and these weren't green hares at all. Ish was, in my eyes, damn near perfect, so exciting to watch with her blood-and-guts style, her fire and determination. But not destined to stay on this earth for long.

Ishtar did miss one hare that day, which came off a field of set-aside and ran over a narrow field of drilling to find sanctuary in a fox hole; she almost had it on the dyke edge before it managed to do a double-bluff turn and slip into the earth. She was back in slips straight away, for the run had not even lasted a minute. Her sides were barely heaving. The second hare jumped from the same field of set-aside, and set off in exactly the same direction as the first had done.

I could see the bitch's ears prick as she realised where the hare was heading: *'I know where you want to go!'* and she angled her run to cut the hare off before it got to the fox hole. Even so, she only just made it, turning hard on the dyke edge, her feet throwing up a spray of damp earth as she lunged, putting all

Ishtar at around one year of age.

her energy into diverting the course of that hare. Dog and hare disappeared down the dyke and someone shouted: "She's got it!"

It was hardly a testing course as such, but a very good example of a dog outwitting a hare on its home ground, ground that the dog hadn't set foot on until that day. Ish hadn't known there was a fox hole in that dyke before the first hare dived to safety, but the innate intelligence of her predator mind recognised instantly that the second hare would attempt the same manoeuvre. I do love a clever dog.

Her third hare that day was a decent slip of around 80 metres, but it went nowhere, forced into a tight-turning error before it had gone a hundred yards. Game over. Ish went on to kill her third later in the afternoon, and it did make her work a bit harder, taking her for over a mile across the fen before she managed to wrap things up. Three out of four on good winter hares. It just wasn't their day. It was the day a clever, quick thinking and fleet-footed little bitch I had bred myself, was just too good for the hares.

Starlight.

How would she have gone on if she'd lived? I'll never know, and I still mourn her passing. She was as good on the lamp as she was on hares, and she loved foxes too. It might be easy to think that only the good die young, and for many years I was convinced that this saying was true. You become paranoid after you've lost a couple of young dogs in freak accidents. It is never easy to lose a dog, but to see a young fit animal die at the height of its powers, its life snuffed out in a second, that really hurts. You begin to ask yourself if it is really all worth it. All the time, the energy, the emotional commitment that you put into the rearing and training of a pup, only to find yourself yet again staring down at the motionless body as it lies, small and sad and all gone.

Yes, I became paranoid, almost too scared to slip my dogs, terrified at night if they ran out of the beam, and each time they ran. For a long while after Ishtar had died, I was tense, as if waiting for yet another accident, but that was before Starlight came along.

The innocent leveret.

INTERLUDE with a Hare

I'VE CALLED this photo The Innocent Leveret, for although three-quarter grown, this particular hare had obviously never seen a human, let alone a dog. Here's how, for a brief spell, I became a 'wildlife photographer'.

One sultry day in June, shortly after a lashing rain storm had swept over the fields, I drove a couple of miles out of my village and up to the farm on what passes for a hill in these parts. There are green lanes, grass tracks and bridleways all over this land, but the hares that I see on these paths are quick to move away when they see you coming; they are used to horses, joggers and mountain bikers, and although seldom chased, they keep their distance. I needed to get a lot closer as I only have a 200ml lens.

So I crept along the edge of a rape field, following the curving boundary, stooping low and hoping to catch an unwary hare as it dried off in the sun. As I rounded the curve on the edge of the field I saw a stretch of grass headland, and there were hares! Seven hares to be precise, about three quarter grown, all engaged in grooming and play. Their fur gleamed damply in the searing light, and I dropped to the ground, flattening myself in the longer grass at the edge of the headland. I crawled, like a stalking leopard, inch by inch, through the thistles and grass, pushing my camera in front of me. Fifty metres, forty, and then thirty. The leverets didn't appear to have noticed me, and the wind blew across my path, carrying my scent away from my quarry.

Still closer I crawled, timing my forward movement with the fluctuating gusts of wind. When the wind dropped I stopped moving; when it rattled the stiff stalks of rape I inched forward; the slight though (to me) deafening rustles of the grass muffled by the louder sound overhead. And so I advanced, each pause followed by a subtle slide forward, until I was a mere three metres from the nearest hare. Eat your heart out David Attenborough! My heart was hammering as hard as if I'd had a dog at my side and was waiting to slip.

But now the long grass was in my way, and I had to sit up to get a clear shot. I rose, inch by imperceptible inch, to my knees and began clicking away, and the hares simply sat there. 'My' hare, the nearest, looked languid and dreamy, though its nearest companions were busy cleaning their ears and feet, occasionally pausing to sniff one another. They must have seen me, and I can only assume that their apparent indifference was due to the fact that they had never been predated by anything or anyone. They simply didn't know fear of other animals, having been born and reared in the safety of their forest of rape, and of course I'd moved so very slowly that maybe I had materialised in a way that hadn't threatened their survival.

I don't know how long I sat there, astonished and thrilled at finding myself so close to such normally timid creatures, but then the sun disappeared behind a black cloud and the wind dropped ominously: more rain was coming. I sat up further, and whilst the leverets didn't panic, they began to move off, obviously unsettled by my presence. It was only when I got home that I realised that I'd had the camera on the wrong setting: the setting for close ups! All that hard work and only one decent photo to show for it: I must practice more!

Seeing hares up close in their natural habitat, without a dog on their tail, just going about their daily business, is something that some hunters never experience; those who view hares as merely a target for their fleet-footed dogs. But I know that true hunters, those who respect and understand their quarry, will understand what I mean when I say that getting close to a wild animal transcends our habitual appreciation for that which we hunt. To paraphrase Surtees, who encapsulates this sentiment entirely when speaking of foxhunting: "it aren't that I loves the hare less, but that I loves the 'ound more". *Handley Cross* (1843)

Venture, first cross Deerhound/Greyhound and grand dam to Starlight: a wonderful dog with tremendous drive and pace though she lacked gears on fen hares.

~ Starlight ~

It is often said that you only ever have one really good dog in a lifetime. I feel very privileged to have shared my hunting life with several dogs which I consider to have been a cut above the rest. Maybe I've been luckier than most, maybe some would say that I'm easily pleased, though I'd disagree with the latter part of that statement. In fact, I'm very critical of my dogs indeed. True, they only have to please me, but as each successive generation comes along, the bar is raised just a little bit more, and subsequent pups have even bigger shoes to fill than the ones that went before.

Starlight had some seriously adept lurchers to live up to, and when I first brought her home, there was nothing in the quiet shy pup to indicate that she'd eventually become my right hand dog, a position she has maintained for most of her life. Even today I still depend on Starlight to lead a pack hunt, and at ten years of age, whilst she may have slowed down a little, she's the one I trust the most to locate prey. Her experience allows her to distinguish the faintest of scents on the air, and her actions and body language speak loudly to the younger dogs, leading them to quest actively for the game that may be quite some distance away. Of course she's by no means my only dog whose drive and enthusiasm makes for an interesting life, but Starlight has always had a core of calm within her; she is a thinker as well as a doer, a most useful attribute when we are hunting as opposed to just chasing.

It is common for prey drive to diminish with age, but most of my own dogs have maintained their interest into old age. Whether this is because they see game, not necessarily catchable, on a

Solar, Starlight's grand sire.

daily basis, thereby keeping them up on their toes and sprightly in mind as well as body, or whether I've just been lucky, I don't know.

The oldsters may no longer be the dogs that are first to the catch, but without their powers of location, their prey sense and field craft, the youngsters would have no one to learn from or follow. As an old dog dies, the young stock are there in the wings, waiting to take the their rightful place.

Starlight was born from a bitch I'd bred from that strange mating between little Solar, the 23 inch coursing dog I've mentioned already, and my old Deerhound/Greyhound. I'd run on two pups from the resulting litter, but sold Starlight's future dam at a year old, mainly because she was showing some sinister traits, so similar to Elka. To be frank, I'd had enough of that anti-social type to last me a lifetime, and when Elka died I swore only to keep dogs which were able to live in harmony with one another.

It is hard work having to keep certain dogs separate because of their canicidal tendencies, and I like an easier life these days. The person that bought her worked her hard on hare for three seasons, then bred from her, using a big red coursing dog from Manchester. I know nothing of his breeding, but the litter these two produced was very mixed indeed, in terms of size and shape.

I ended up taking two pups from this litter, Starlight, and a dog pup, which I called Rhino. For reasons unknown, his dam had tried to kill him at birth, ripping the newborn pup's skin like tissue paper on front and hind legs and along his flank. The vets managed to save him, and Rhino was put on a Labrador bitch which had lost her pups. He healed just fine, but bore long, bald scars on his legs and flank for the rest of his life. The Labrador reared him until he was nearly seven weeks of age when he went back to join the rest of the litter to be sold. We often joked that as an 'only' pup, he'd received more than his fair share of milk, and some of the Labrador bulk as well, which accounted for his great size and strength.

Rhino was the canine equivalent of a warhorse! He grew to 29 inches at the shoulder, had a head like a bucket, and a chest like the keel of an ocean-going yacht. He was massively built in every sense, and moved with the grace of Muhammad Ali in his younger days. He could stay forever, was the only dog I've owned who could dispatch a fox with one mighty shake of his head, and was one of the nicest dogs I've ever known.

Poor Rhino, he dislocated his hip at only two years of age and had to be put down. I was gutted. I'd loved that dog completely and utterly, never a good thing to do with working dogs, whose lives can be over in the blink of an eye. You'd have thought I'd have known better than to give my all to a lurcher by the time Rhino came along.

Nowadays, I begin to worry if I see one of my pups acting too perfect and knowledgeable at an early age. Rhino, and bear in mind he was almost all sighthound, was doing down-stays and drops at a distance with hand signals by the time he was six months of age. At a year old he was jumping hedges which would have made a racehorse baulk. In short, he never put a foot wrong until the day he slammed sideways into a tin bath hidden in brambles as he pursued a muntjac through cover, and tore the ball-joint of his hip from its socket. The resulting ligament damage was too severe to repair in a dog of his size and weight, and I wouldn't have consigned him to a life as a pet on the end of a lead.

Now I like pups which have to learn things slowly. I actually welcome the pups which test my patience or those which seem dreamy and quiet with no drive or punch in their natures. I've too often found that the 'perfect' puppies, those who mature early to become almost perfect adults; those that know their quarry too well too soon, are those which are seldom destined to stay on this earth for long.

'Angel dogs' the gypsies sometimes call them; too wise, too young and too gifted from the start. They are the old souls who've been here before and don't need to stay long in their present life on this earth. I'm not at all religious, but I've known quite a few of these dogs, and their lives have always been cut short by freak accidents. I'm forced to believe that some greater power is at work when yet another supremely gifted and precocious youngster is plucked from life ... or am I just trying to make sense of senseless accidents?

Luckily, or unluckily, whichever way you like to look at it, I'm a slow learner, and I continue to offer my "heart to a dog to tear", as Rudyard Kipling, the novelist and poet, warned us against. He must have known from personal experience just how hard it hits when you lose a dog which has been at your side for many years. Losing an old dog is sad, but to lose a youngster at the start of its career is much, much worse. The sense of unfairness I feel when a young dog dies is immense, and I rail against the injustice of death with an anger that consumes me for weeks and weeks after the loss.

Having said that, I'd never be able to get so much from my hounds if I was forever peering sideways, afeared of the shadow of death as it hovers in the background, waiting to claim its next victim. You have to let your dogs live their lives, and keeping them on the lead or wrapped in cotton wool denies them their birthright. Of course, there's a fine line to be drawn between letting a pup do too much, and that of giving it the correct amount of exposure in the field as it grows up. The best working dogs have been reared in the field, so to speak, seeing quarry commensurate with their abilities at any given age.

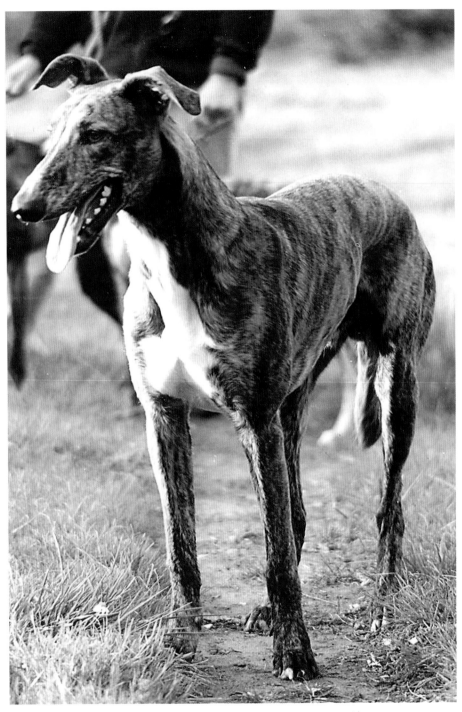

Rhino, a giant of a dog.

If Rhino had lived to fulfil his potential, I would maybe have been writing about him instead of his sister. It wasn't to be. Starlight, the apparently timid and shy little sister, grew up almost unnoticed, so in love was I with her big, fine brother. She played happily by herself or with her brother; she occupied her puppyhood by chasing rabbits and squirrels, and lay quietly at home, unassuming, but slowly developing the confidence which would later enable her to become the mainstay of my pack.

She wouldn't be trained! She wouldn't do down-stays or hidden retrieves. She hated water and sulked on the end of the lead, but she always came when called, and didn't indulge in those infuriating games that some pups play as they push you to the limits of patience. And she never ran off. She was just there, minding her own business, and quietly evolving into something which would one day prove very useful indeed.

I find that some Saluki-type lurchers are strange when they're young. They seem remote, not properly switched on, and definitely not as responsive as you'd expect a puppy to be. It is a big mistake to assume that such pups are stupid or 'not all there'. They are 'there' all right, just not in the way that we expect of a domestic dog.

These pups are almost feral in their attitude, seeming to live their lives on a parallel plane to the rest of us, until one day everything seems to slot into place and they take their rightful position at your side. It's almost as though they don't recognise the importance of the human who feeds them, and it is only once you take them out working, just the two of you, that they suddenly understand that this slow and clumsy human just might bear some importance in their lives.

I truly believe that these Saluki-minded pups have brains which mature in a different way to most other types of dog; they're a throwback to those independent creatures of the desert, which live only to hunt. In the desert there are no boundaries, no fences and walls, and most native-bred pups can wander at will, unfettered by a kennel environment. This could be why many Saluki-type pups resist being kennelled or confined; they find it unbearable to be thus imprisoned, their plaintive howls splitting the air as their protests drive you mad!

OK, so I'm probably being fanciful again! But how else can I explain the strange and remote natures of these pups, and the fact that some can only begin to gel with their human once they are old enough to work in the field? Sure, these pups have a hunting brain from the first days they leave the nest. You only have to watch them stalking and catching grasshoppers in the garden, or waiting intently, cat-like, for the unwary sparrow to land just that inch too close to their motionless paws.

But that's just it, these pups live to hunt, from far too early an age, if you let them. Beware of letting a six-month-old Saluki-saturated lurcher do its own thing in the field. If you want to play an active part in the life of a Saluki lurcher, you have to make yourself indispensable to them. One of the reasons so many pet (and some working) lurcher owners have problems with recall is that these people simply take their pup out for a walk, let it off the lead and then proceed to take no further part in the activity.

If you plod along admiring the view, ignoring your hound and

Starlight and Andy getting a mark with the old grey box.

generally acting in a fashion which elicits no need for response from your pup you can bet your life that the youngster will eventually tire of running circles around you in an effort to generate some excitement. All too soon its nose will lead it to things which are much more interesting than you'll ever be, and it's off, deaf to your startled cries.

Softlee softlee, catchee monkey, or, in this case, catchee dog. I've made the mistake of trying to over-train many different types of pups before I knew better. And I've seen the result of over-training in other people's dogs as well. Take the brilliant Collie-bred lurcher which was winning obedience competitions up and down the country before it was a year old. By the time this youngster was 15 months of age she was refusing to even pick up a dummy, so sickened was she by the endless discipline and repeated routines. I've heard that she went on to become a useful working dog in the field, and I may well be speaking out of turn

Starlight divided single-handed with J. Bellerby and Mac (runner-up).

here in seeming to criticise her trainer, but I feel strongly that pups should be allowed to be pups; they need a certain degree of freedom to evolve into competent and willing adults. Mind you, I've always been against forcing hard-core intellectual education down the throats of young human beings as well, and I believe that such early academic cramming of young minds often results in much more serious rebellion when they hit the terrible teens.

In my opinion, a young dog should spend the first year of its life learning about the things that it would naturally encounter in what will eventually be its working world, with the exception of challenging quarry of course. I do little serious obedience training apart from basic recall and lead training, with a couple of fun retrieves thrown in once or twice a week. Anyway, enough pontificating on dogs, I'm supposed to be talking about Starlight!

She spent the first two winters of her life coursing hares, though in truth, I ran her only a little that first season. She wasn't yet strong enough for those savvy, well-coursed beasts. That strength and blistering speed which I loved so much would come in her second winter.

Some pups just don't seem to show any sparks of greatness until they actually start working. Then, suddenly, or so it seems, that drive and brain, those skills and traits which have been simmering quietly, maturing gently like a slow-cooked stew, explode into life with a vengeance. One's mind plays tricks of course, and I must have seen something in Starlight which warranted the patient approach. Call it instinct or merely a glimpse of a spark yet to be ignited in that marvellous head.

When I first ran her with the club, people said that she'd only be a sprinter, not a stayer. "She's too fast to stay on", they said. Her thigh muscles were more those of a Greyhound than a Saluki-type. But she did stay, quite enough to catch the majority of the hares that she ran and her drive was superb. Hers might not have been quite the stamina of the pure Saluki, but it was every bit enough to catch most of the hares she ran.

Starlight has huge, shining eyes which are set in her skull like great orbs of glowing light. I've never known a dog able to convey so much meaning with just one glance, and she bonded with me, her human counterpart, with whom she could share her zest for life, for the hunt. I feel honoured to have shared my hunting life with such a dog.

Although she was a good hare dog, learning to run her hares quickly and well, it was always that brain which gave her the edge, the ability to know instinctively where the hare was trying to go. Mistakes on the part of the hares always led to their quick demise, for this bitch was blessed with a damn near perfect strike as well. Hares caught quickly, often at a dyke side as they attempted to leave the field, seldom made that leap, for Starlight was there, side-swiping their jump. Those hares would be carried back to me at a gallop, then thrown contemptuously at my feet, often still alive, and I had to be quick to get hold of both hare and dog, for the bitch would be up on her toes again, and looking about for her next victim.

I remember when she caught four out of four on the second day of the single-handed final, equalling the tally of the bitch with which we decided to split the trophy. It wasn't the outcome I wanted, and she'd only managed one out of three on the first day of the final, two days previously. That had partly been due to my stupid slipping on impossible hares which jumped too far and headed for cover before the dog had got into her stride. I told you I was a rubbish slipper when it came to competition! I would have liked to run a third day to settle any doubts completely, but the rules forbade us to carry on running another day, and to be honest, I'd had enough of the endless bickering within the competition: was that slip too short? Should it count or not? Or did the dog actually turn the hare before it went into cover, so should it really constitute a course or not? It is hard to be laid-back and philosophical about such things when you desperately wanted to win!

Starlight's first and second hares were picked up very quickly, but the third, a long swinging hare and a good 80 yard slip, almost wiped her out on the run-up. It leapt a big dyke and the bitch, galloping hard to get on terms with it, missed her footing as she leapt to soar over the abyss beneath her feet. For a heart-stopping moment I had visions of another broken-back accident as the lurcher somersaulted on the far edge of the steep bank. She got shakily to her feet, and although she'd lost a lot of ground, and seemed to be running awkwardly as she set off again, she

140

ploughed along, gaining speed as she ran in the wake of the hare which was fast approaching a mound of rubbish surrounded by the remains of pheasant cover. Only that tremendous will drove her on, determined to keep her prey in view, but they both disappeared behind the mound and I thought that the hare was lost. Those interminable moments that pass as you watch and wait, too far away to run and find out what is happening. You stand, motionless, praying that your dog is all right, wondering if the course of a lifetime is happening in the distance, out of your sight.

Then Starlight reappeared, trotting through the long grass carrying her hare. It might not have been the most stylish course in the world, nor the longest, though I have it down in my diary as standing at three and half minutes, thanks to one of the club members who carried a stopwatch wherever he went. Still, a decent length run, and for sheer guts and determination it took some beating. Her fourth hare jumped on heavy plough, and she seemed to make hard work of it, probably by now stiff and sore from her fall, but she nailed it after a run lasting two and a half minutes. She might have had another run in her that day, but I was wary of running the bitch again, and secretly pleased that the decision was made to divide the trophy. John B's bitch had run well over both days and either dog would have made a worthy winner.

I've never bothered timing my dogs' runs, but it's sometimes useful to know just how long it takes for a dog to catch a good winter hare on strange ground. When a dog runs hares on land it knows like the back of its paw, the odds can be stacked in favour of the dog, rather than the hare, for the dog knows which routes the hares are likely to take in their race for survival and run to cut them off.

Good, experienced dogs read the land around them when running, even if they've never set foot on those fields before. This takes practice, though many of the purpose-bred hare dogs seem to be born 'hare savvy', instinctively realising that hares will always make for cover, be that hedge, wood or dyke. Predators read their prey's body language as it runs, noticing every detail of how the ears lay on the hare: are they flat to its back or upright? Does that flick of one ear indicate what the hare is thinking as it runs? And dogs notice when the hare looks confused, or panicky, thrown from its chosen route.

I didn't start lamping Starlight until after the ban came in. Her life before that was always hares, with the odd fox thrown in for good measure.

She took to the lamp like the proverbial duck to water, and her experience with hares led her to run round a rabbit heading straight for the hedge. She boxed them away from their homes, and picked them up all too easily. Rabbits were a cinch compared to the twisting, jinking hares she'd been used to. Rabbits may be quick over a short distance, but they tend to run in straight lines, turn sharply then straight line again. Starlight thought they were great, though she'd not pick a squatter. She tried that once, and failed, so forever after she'd stand almost on top of a sitting rabbit, waiting for it to jump. Once it jumped, she knew then which way it was heading, and her great thrust and drive usually caught the rabbit before it had gone more than a few yards. She really did make it look too easy.

Rabbits kept Starlight simmering along nicely, but they were just bread and butter work, and didn't really 'do it' for her. Her main goal in life was to rid her land of foxes.

A nice brace on the Fens, bolted and shot.

It's a funny thing about dogs and foxes. So often, the dog you think wouldn't look at a fox turns out to be a demon killer of rusty red vermin. So it was with Starlight. Her first fox, taken at around two years of age as the terriers put it out of cover on one of our daily mooches, made the mistake of biting her as she grabbed it, not unnaturally, and she immediately lost her temper! With a roar of outrage she piled into the unfortunate vulpine, killing it in seconds. From that moment on she was hell on legs, bent on extracting every ounce of revenge on every fox she met. Age and arthritis have slowed this lurcher's body a little, but she still lives each day on a mission to find the next fox, hunting continuously through cover the moment she gets on a scent, following on with her nose to the trail like a foxhound. Her muzzle bears scars both ancient and fresh, testimony to her continued drive, ambition and success. There are no second chances for a fox once Starlight has got it in her sights.

I did think once, during a particularly ferocious battle early on in her career with a huge dog fox she'd found one day, that she'd grown wary, or that she lacked bottle, for instead of securing her prey with her normally efficient throat or neck hold, she danced warily round in a circle, dibbing and dabbing at the fox as it snapped and uttered its guttural challenge. The terriers caught up with the action and finished the job whilst I drooped in despair, until I checked the lurcher's mouth and found that she'd put both upper canine teeth through her lips in the struggle: a case of literally biting her own lips.

People who used lurchers to take fox on a regular basis will know what I mean, but it is a weird sight to see two fangs protruding from halfway up the dog's lips. You have to be decisive and pull the lip firmly downwards to slide it off the end of the tooth. Some more insensitive dogs may be able to maintain their death grip despite such a painful handicap, but you have to remember that Starlight was a 'mere' Saluki-type lurcher, not a hard bitten Bull type. Gashes to the face she could handle, but to be handicapped by her own fangs was more than she could take. Luckily, this has only happened twice in her life to date.

One of the most memorable 'takes' happened on the Lincolnshire fens. We were on a dig in a dyke side, as usual, and the fox bolted, leapt the dyke and tore off down the edge of the field on the opposite side. One hundred yards away the dyke turned sharp left. Instead of leaping the dyke and following the exact line of the fox, Starlight galloped the length of the field, keeping almost parallel to her quarry as it bolted down the far side of the dyke. The fox, running down the deep furrow at the edge of the plough, turned left to follow the direction of the dyke, and at precisely the moment it came across Starlight's sights, like a bullet she took a direct path through the air, over the dyke and collided with the fox. (This was one of the larger drainage ditches, though not large enough to be called a drain. It was probably around 12 feet across from top of bank to top of bank.)

I don't think that she actually thought this one through before she took off, for the impact threw the fox up into the air, along with the dog, which cart-wheeled across the plough to land in a muddy wet heap. The bitch leapt back to her feet, as soon as she landed, and flung herself on the disorientated animal, and both disappeared from sight into the dyke bottom. I heard Starlight's customary howl of anger as the fox retaliated, and by the time we'd clumsily staggered across the plough (you try running across deep, fresh plough!) she had the situation under control.

That was Starlight all over. Whilst she is sensitive and intelligent, she goes into a type of Viking 'berserker zone' when she comes up on a fox. Such is her need to get to grips with her sworn enemy that she throws caution to the winds and usually ends up with yet another scar on her head to mark the occasion. I could go on waxing lyrical about this bitch all day, and endlessly describe the many foxes she's killed in her life, but it is the moments of real communication between us, especially those which have led to the successful conclusion of a hunt, which stand out more in my mind than the mere blood-and-guts battles with toothy prey.

I've already described the day when Starlight told me where Sonic had gone to ground in the 'Swiss cheese' bank, finding, among literally hundreds of burrows, exactly the entrance to where the fox and dog would be found. This next account might seem to some not extraordinary at all, but it demonstrates the empathy we have together, me and my right hand dog, and how we know each other. I've never had such a feeling of camaraderie with a dog before, and at the risk of sounding anthropomorphic, I see a glint of mischievous glee in her eyes when she communicates the impending excitement for the hunt.

We were walking back to my van after our normal afternoon's exercise. I say exercise, but I'm fortunate inasmuch that even our daily walks allow the dogs to indulge in a fair amount of hunting round cover and fields of set-aside. As we headed for home along a high bank covered in thistles and weeds, I could hear the sound of the rush-hour traffic roaring above my head on that chill November evening. It was dusk, and the temperature was dropping fast. I'd leashed up the terriers as I negotiated the steep incline, knowing full well that at this time of year the odd fox might have slipped into one of the many old rabbit warrens which littered the slopes.

To my left lay a flat, gravelled expanse, then a large mound of earth the size of at least two buses all covered in brambles, then a lake. The lakes round here are really old gravel pits, now full of water and teeming with aquatic life. A collection of coots paddled peacefully on the water, occasionally dispersed by the resident swans who didn't take kindly to lesser birds invading their patch. The wind whooshed and whistled through the beds of tall reeds in the glimmering cold shadows; winter was on its way.

The lurchers trudged behind me, satisfied with the brace of bunnies we'd caught on the lake margins, but Starlight was questing: something on the breeze, some faint scent had caught her sensitive nostrils. She trotted ahead of me, suddenly alert once more, lifting her head, turning to catch the slightest trace of a smell which had lifted her mind from the boring trudge home.

Now she's up on her toes, and running towards the edge of the bank, looking, sniffing and darting from side to side. She's like a locator, tuning in to the exact spot from whence the scent is flowing; flowing invisible to the eye, but present in waves which grow stronger and stronger at each pass of the head, each step in the right direction.

Finally, she stops right on the edge of the bank, and she's looking across at the thorn-covered mound not 20 feet to our left. She turns and looks at me, and her great eyes are shining with anticipation. She looks at the brambles again, then turns her head to stare into my eyes. *'There's a fox in there.'* So obvious is her message that she might as well have spoken out loud. I honestly wouldn't be surprised to hear this dog speak!

It's the wrong time of day, it is cold and I want to go home and light a good fire in the hearth and snuggle down for the night, but how can I refuse those eyes, that pleading intensity from a dog which lives for the hunt. And I can't ignore the mounting excitement inside me either! We're the same, Starlight and I, we both live for those moments. There is in both of us a fanatical need to seek out and hunt our quarry. And those moments are so much better when they happen out of the blue, unexpectedly shifting mundane exercise into a different gear.

Though the kill is important, the actual finding, the hunt and subsequent chase holds an equal importance to me, which is why I don't shoot. I could go out at night and shoot foxes and rabbits by the barrowful, but it wouldn't mean anything to me at all. I'm sure that dogs are the same. Their energy is charged with the prospect of hunting, and although that energy grounds itself in the kill, it is better to hunt and lose their quarry than not to hunt at all.

Starlight looks mischieviously at me.

I let temptation get the better of me, and despite my misgivings, knowing that a fox flushed now might well lead to a terrier deep underground, I release Midge from the couple. "Get on there", I say, though she needs no encouragement at all, for she too has caught that scent; she's been standing on her hind feet trying desperately to reach those invisible particles on the air flowing across just inches above her head. She knows too, from experience just where to go. She's worked this mound on many occasions for rabbits, but she's also flushed muntjac and fox from the place in the past.

Midge scuttles down the bank and disappears into the encroaching pile of brambles, and the lurchers fan out along the bank, trying to cover as much of the ground as possible. We stand and listen, though the rustle of the terrier's progress is hidden by the sound of the wind, but I soon hear a yap, then another and another, and a big red blur leaps airborne as the fox bolts vertically from its hiding place, straight up out of the middle of the bramble on the mound.

The lurchers galvanise into action and Starlight jumps straight down the bank. She's right on the fox as it twists and turns, using each broken branch and bramble stem as cover in its flight for freedom. And now it's running straight towards me, and I let out a groan as it flashes to ground in a hole at the base of the bank, and Midge has gone straight in after it.

I check my phone for the time. Andy should be home by now, and once again I shall have to call him and ask him very nicely to come out with a spade, locator and Midge's retired dam, Sonic. I really do try not to let the terriers go to ground round here, where the banks are big, the earths may be deeper than coal mines, and certainly not at this time of day! But once again, I have responded to that calling, that plea from my dog, and once again, we're sitting outside an earth on a cold, damp evening when normal people are tucking up warm in their houses. Andy sounds resigned, he's more used to this scenario than he should be, and within half an hour he's climbing the bank, equipped for a dig.

"Can you hear her?" he asks, referring to Midge.

"Just a bit of baying and the odd bump," I reply. I collar up Sonic, who is peering myopically into the earth with cloudy eyes.

Each time I retire her she gets called into action once more. She's over ten years old now, and her eyes have born the brunt of a lifetime's work in cover and to ground, but her nose is still as acute as it was as a pup. She disappears into the inky blackness of the hole, and we wait. I've tied up most of the lurchers to branches and trees, leaving just Starlight loose to patrol the many holes which surround 'the hole', the one where fox and terrier had entered. As luck would have it, the locator leads Andy to the depths of a big old bramble on the side of the bank; he mutters something in disgust.

"What?" I ask. "15 feet" comes the snorted answer.

It can't be; no way! But Andy is now under the bramble, heaving through the myriad woody stems, cursing and slipping, grunting with effort and sounding like an old badger rooting for grubs in the mud. It starts to rain. Then he's out the other side of the bramble, just under a small tree, and I can feel the relief flooding towards me as he says:

"Four feet now".

Thank God for that! The mark holds steady and I pass him the spade. As it turns out, it's less than four feet, barely three, and the sandy soil of the gravely bank gives easily, soon exposing the terrier, first Sonic, whiffling and squeaking at her daughter's rear. We lift her out, and soon Midge is in sight, lugging on something unseen though she can barely breathe, so tight is the tunnel.

Andy pulls Midge from the soil with difficulty, having first scraped the sand from its deadly embrace round her flanks, and there lies the fox, and it's not moving at all. Driven head first to the stop end it is stone dead and unmoving, suffocated in the loose sand of the tight tube it sought as sanctuary. I feel a sense of loss, of disappointment. Starlight feels it too, and nudges the fox hopefully. Its mouth is full of sand. It never stood a chance.

I often ask myself just why I feel this way when we've dug to a dead fox, something which does happen on occasion in these sandy places. It's almost as though we've been cheated, which I know is a stupid thought. Nevertheless, whilst we want the fox to be dead at the culmination of a hunt, it somehow seems wrong for death to occur in such a way. As though the terrier has been denied the opportunity to test its mettle face to face with its foe as it should. Still, it wasn't the terrier's fault that the fox couldn't or wouldn't turn to face her, and the farmer over the road with his little rough shoot wouldn't care how the fox died, just that one more pheasant-killer was accounted for. I pat Starlight's head. She's not interested in ragging a dead thing, though Sonic and Midge have to be dragged from their enjoyment. We bury the carcase quickly and head back for the van as the rain turns to sleet.

~ SOME THOUGHTS ON FOXES ~

Whilst I appreciate that foxes need to be strictly controlled on sheep farms or game shoots, my own attitude to that fellow predator has become slightly more ambivalent in recent years. The killing of an animal for which I have no personal use is harder to justify … but here's the rub: I love my dog work too, and so I must live with that conflict within me.

For me, hunting is all about providing me and my dogs with food, and whilst some brave people say that they've eaten fox, I've never been remotely tempted to consume an animal which smells as pungent as our vulpine co-predators.

I also have the greatest respect for predators of any kind. Their lives are far harder than that of a prey animal, which only has to open its jaws and browse the grass or vegetation beneath its feet. The fox must stalk and catch its prey using skill and a canny brain, going hungry if it fails in that attempt.

Sure, I know that foxes eat more or less anything they can swallow when times are hard. When I find fox scats full of green, undigested and unripe sloes during summer, I realise just how hard it is for young foxes to survive in a land of seeming plenty. When myxomatosis strikes in summer those youngsters must surely stand a better chance of living to adulthood, but times have been hard of late, and in recent years the only outbreaks of myxie have been in early spring or autumn. These are the times when I find fox droppings full of all sorts of indigestible material, testimony to their desperate attempts to ward off starvation.

One late spring my dogs found a vixen, full in milk and skeletal with it. Her gums and tongue were white and bloodless, her coat sparse and thin, though not mangy. She was out in broad daylight, staggering weakly along a footpath, and she died instantly, a merciful death which cut short her obvious suffering. I knew the location of her cubs, and for a full two months after that vixen died, I daily brought butcher's scraps and the odd dead rabbit to the earth, knowing that the over-night disappearance of my offerings meant the cubs were surviving. The earth was near a nature reserve, and no one had shoots in the area, so I had no qualms about aiding those small fellow predators in their bid for survival.

Later on that summer, I wasn't surprised to see large and healthy young foxes along the same hedgerows and I like to think that my actions had given them the start they needed. I have never had any wish to kill foxes for the sake of it, and I've often watched them hunting during the long summer evenings.

I remember once seeing a vixen near the old landfill site. She was sitting, like a rust-coloured statue, immobile and patient, just on the edge of a bramble. A few yards behind her sat a cub the size of a large cat; it watched the vixen with the same intent that she watched the bramble. I called the dogs to heel (luckily a thick growth of thistles had hidden the foxes from their sight) and crept away, not wishing to disturb the pair, and continued my walk.

I meandered back along the same path half an hour later, and was just in time to see the vixen disappearing over the landfill mound, a rabbit hanging from her jaws, whilst the cub danced eagerly round her in hungry delight.

Other times I've disturbed foxes as they hunted, and whilst I try to keep the dogs from them in summer, accidents do happen on occasion. Many years ago, we were heading towards a grass field in June, and the hay had not yet been cut. As we approached the open gateway a fox, carrying a rabbit in its jaws, crossed our path, not 60 yards ahead, and the lurchers leapt forward, blasting through the opening in a manic and ill-thought out attack, just as the fox vanished into the long grass to the right of the gate. As the dogs sped out into the field, I watched as the fox reappeared, looked quickly in the direction the dogs had gone, and slipped back along its original path before working its way quietly and calmly up the railway embankment to my left. I called the dogs back and admonished them for their brainless antics, though I had to feel pleased that I wouldn't have to bear the guilt associated with killing a fellow predator during its breeding season.

A fox which entered my garden and destroyed my flock of bantams was a different matter! It's funny how our subjective views on animals are apt to change when our own domestic possessions are threatened, and had I been able to, I'd have killed that fox by any means available to me, whilst mourning the scattered corpses of my speckledy strain of Old English Game hybrids. That particular villain never returned for the corpses it had left in the pen, and so avoided the strategically placed snare we set in the fence.

I guess I've had a love-hate relationship with foxes ever since, as a small child, I woke up one morning to find that my beautiful Belgian Hare had been dragged from her hutch by a fox. Now, for the most part, I tend to see foxes as a worthy, if inedible, quarry, though I wish I had the time and the patience to make use of their pelts; if that were the case I'd feel that their deaths were less of a waste.

I think that many hunters soften their attitudes later in life, becoming more tolerant, less desperate to mete out death to every fox they see. Or does our prey drive diminish along with advancing age, where we are constantly reminded of our own mortality?

Unfortunately, pack-caught fox pelts are unusable, and though I did at one time attempt to cure several skins, they ended up languishing in my freezer for months before being thrown out. Tanning pelts is a laborious and time-consuming process, and one which I've just never got around to completing. It's not as if I actually need the skins to clothe myself, though I harboured dreams of a fox fur bedspread for many a year!

One year we did feed a couple of full grown foxes to two very hungry litters of ferret kits, and whilst the jills were understandably nervous, 16 kits demolished an entire carcase over a 24-hour period, and with no ill effects. The second one proved just as tasty a meal to those kits, but we did make sure that those foxes weren't showing any signs of mange. To be honest, I've only once come across a mangy fox in this area, which is a blessing considering how many there are.

Dumped foxes are beginning to show up all too regularly, and it is easy to identify them as they are usually very well fed, and obviously strangers to the area. When a fox runs instantly in

At 11 years old and still keen!

the wrong direction, leaving itself open to attack, you immediately realise that it has no idea of where to find cover or safety. We often find several over a period of two or three days, and they are always laid up in the most unsuitable and dangerous (for both foxes and me) places, such as right next to well-used tracks and paths.

I have, on more than one occasion, been forced to adopt the 'shocked dog walker' approach when these accidents threatened to land me in trouble! Crying in a high pitched voice: "Oh you naughty dogs!" whilst muttering encouragement under my breath, I've had to appear distraught and overwhelmed at the vulpicidal tendencies of my dogs when a dog walker or jogger has appeared round a bend in the path, right at the moment my dastardly doggies have ploughed into a tiny bramble intent on killing such a fox.

Sometimes it really helps to be a woman in this sort of situation, and I'm not ashamed to admit that I've used the 'little woman' approach on more than one occasion to absolve myself of any part in an unintentional vulpicidal attack.

One such occasion springs to mind ...

~ THE HAPLESS DOG WALKER ~

I was just unloading the dogs from my van preparatory to our daily walk, and as usual I'd let the terriers out first because the hatch to the built in terrier box acts as a step down for the lurchers in their cages on top of the box. Normally, the only things to be found in the straggly patch of brambles just inside the gateway were rabbits, but before I'd had time to release the lurchers, a cacophony of baying broke the peace of that sunny afternoon. That wasn't a rabbit baying sound at all!

I should explain that I'd parked on the side of a small dead-end lane, where each day, many dog walkers gathered to exercise their various mutts. On the far side of the lane stood two elderly women, garbed in what passes for country wear amongst town dwellers. Brightly coloured wellies, shiny green plastic macs, and head scarves of the type so beloved of members of the Royal Family: so were these women attired, and their small, obese terrier thingies were decked out in green wax-proof, tartan-lined coats, despite the unseasonably warm weather. I think we were in early February, but like so many of the weird winters we have in the East of England, the sun often shines whilst other parts of the country are suffering a deluge of freezing rain or sleet.

These details I registered in a panic stricken flash, a glance which took in my immediate surroundings as I assessed the risk of being accused of having murderous, dangerous dogs in a public place. I did the only sensible thing I could think of doing ... I released Starlight from the van, leaving the other lurchers whining softly in frustration.

Starlight flew to the source of the baying, which had now become grunting and growling, and I thanked God that the unseen prey hadn't been a muntjac, whose eerie screams would be splitting the air by now. All noise ceased as the lurcher arrived on the invisible scene, though I could see the brambles and leaves trembling above the reality beneath. I started to call the dogs out, knowing full well that they weren't listening, but for the benefit of the watching women across the road I was using that fed up voice you hear all the time from dog walkers who know that they've no control whatsoever over their dogs.

"Oh Midge, please come here", I begged, raising my voice just a little, trying to sound as though this happened all the time.

Rabbits are great!

Squeaky voice now, raised an octave or so: "Bad dog Midge, come out of there, right now!"

I risked a glance over the road, where the two women were looking my way with far too much interest and not a little concern. They weren't to know that I'd never have spoken to my dogs in that manner: I have never felt such an idiot, but needs must to avert any suspicion that I might actually have dogs that did this all the time and knew exactly what they were doing.

"Are you all right, dear?" one of them called, no doubt alerted by the initial volley of barks and none too subtle growls which had subsequently filtered from the depths of the bramble. "Do you need some help?"

Errm, no! No way did I want any help at all thank you very much! I thought fast, and fear lent me words which would conjure up an acceptable image to the dog-owning public, I hoped!

"It's all right", I called back, trying to sound bored and slightly annoyed with my dogs, as though this sort of thing happened all the time. "They've caught a rabbit in the bramble and they're just arguing over it."

Right answer! The helpful women subsided, obviously relieved that I didn't want to take them up on their offer of help. I doubt they'd have known what to do if I'd welcomed that offer anyway, and the thought of dogs fighting each other obviously didn't appeal to them one little bit. Of course, they weren't fighting each other at all, just venting their spleen on what was probably already a carcase.

I love rabbits. Rabbits are great! They are an acceptable thing for a dog to chase; all dogs chase rabbits, even those fat little, tartan-clad pets on the ends of their shiny leads were to be seen rocking along unsteadily in the wake of a bunny from time to time. Rabbits are fair game for all dogs. Rabbits have got me out of trouble on more than one occasion.

The plastic-covered pair went their merry way, and I set about extricating terriers from bramble. The fox was of course by now an ex-fox, and Starlight looked up at me, smug satisfaction written all over her blood-stained face. As usual, she'd sustained a nick or two, and her head sprouted dozens of thorns, but luckily we weren't far from water, and I would be sure to plunge her head in the lake when we got there to remove the shocking evidence of the kill, which had made her look like something from an anti-vivisection film.

As I tucked the large fox under the leaves out of sight, I couldn't help noticing that not only was it almost obese, but that most of its teeth were missing, including its fangs. There was no way such a creature would have been able to live so well with most of its weaponry gone. And the fact that it had been laid up in a bramble not yards from a car park was evidence enough for me to assume that it had probably been dumped by some wildlife charity very recently indeed, maybe only that morning.

I see red when I find evidence of this kind of misguided and so called 'charitable' activity. So many of the people involved in rescuing and saving wildlife have no real idea of what a wild animal needs in terms of habitat. Foxes are territorial animals, they need to grow up and learn how to live in their environments from an early age. When adult foxes are deposited into a habitat

Four dumped foxes bolted from a drain near a chicken farm.

of which they have no local knowledge, they find it much harder to survive, and if they're dumped next to chicken farms (yes, I've seen it happen!) or where domestic animals are not well protected, they'll take the easy route to a free lunch rather than waste energy hunting wild and switched-on rabbits.

I realise that I'm preaching to the converted in saying all this in a book which is highly unlikely to be read by anyone other than fellow hunters, but say it I must, in the vague hope that some germs of sense might percolate by an extremely unlikely route to those other ears.

Two of my original Lakelands, Pig and Storm. Hard hitters below ground but less useful as part of a pack: as the saying goes, it's horses for courses!

~ Terrier Tales ~

Although my hunting life has been centred on lurchers more than other types of dog, I couldn't write a book on my dogs without devoting a chapter to the terriers. It has often been said that you are either a terrier man who keeps lurchers, or a lurcher man who keeps terriers; one type of dog always taking precedence over the other. Never a truer word was said, for there are very few people who genuinely have the time, the interest, the energy or indeed the means, to give to both types of dogs the amount of work that merits the title of genuine worker.

I fall into the second category (albeit in female form), and although I used to do a fair amount of digging at one time, when my body was younger and stronger than it is today, my first love has always been lurchers. I look wistfully back over the years and wonder how I managed to fit everything into those winter months; working full time, lamping two, if not three, times a week when the moon was down, and coursing each Saturday, (often midweek as well as after the end of the shooting season) whilst Sundays were fox-digging days. I even managed to fit in a spot of ferreting now and again. No wonder I'm now a crippled old wreck ... but I wouldn't have changed those crazy, driven years for anything!

Whilst the lurchers have usually taken centre stage, our lives, both theirs and mine, would have been poorer by far had we not worked in tandem with those extraordinary little tykes, those mini heat-seeking missiles on legs whose sole aim in life is to track each scent to its source and to flush or kill.

Lurchers seldom get the chance to hunt up successfully on rough, open ground if you live on the flat arable land of East

Anglia, unless we're talking about hares of course, though in recent years those strange and fluffy-eared, doe-eyed interlopers from China (Chinese Water Deer) have been steadily increasing in number. Like the hare, they are apt to spring up from the middle of a beet field, where they've lain tight amidst foliage which you'd have thought too short to conceal more than a mouse.

The wildlife is either to ground or hidden tight in the odd spinneys and hedgerows, or pheasant cover, which of course is verboten to lurchers and terriers except on shoot days. The only exceptions to this are the over-grown dyke sides ... if you are lucky, and the farmer hasn't flailed all the growth from the steep sided banks.

If I waited for organised days out beating on shoots, my dogs would see very little day time work on open ground through the winter, so I guess I'm doubly lucky to have access to some rather neglected land which is not shot over; land where the humble rabbit is our main quarry, though there are plenty of surprise

Midge and Beetle.

guests to be found from time to time. Rabbits, however, are the bread and butter of our daily lives and they keep the dogs busy and reasonably fit throughout the year.

"Terriers for rabbiting?" I hear some say ...

"Why not?" I reply. Why not indeed! I expect my lurchers to multi-task, so why not my terriers? Dyed-in-the-wool earthdog men scoff at the idea of allowing a terrier to work rabbits above ground, but terriers can and will do both jobs, and my terriers never go to ground on rabbit either. Some people might find that impossible to believe. They think that a terrier which wants to go to ground will surely follow a rabbit when it dives into a burrow. Maybe some lines of terrier are like that. All I can say is that mine don't, and never have done, whether they've been Russell-types or the black and tan Lakies I used to keep.

Sure, as little pups of four or five months old, their noses lead them to investigate each hole they come across. If I come across a pup which is intent on trying to get into a rabbit hole, I pull it out, pick it up and carry it for a few yards until that particular hole is behind us. If you are fortunate enough to find sufficient rabbits in cover, terriers soon learn that rabbits are hunted on top, and never to ground. Conditioning has everything to do with this. If you never, ever dig out a rabbit which the dogs have marked, they soon learn that this isn't their role in life.

Conversely, if you don't have many rabbits in your area, and you hang around each hole when the dogs show an interest, you can expect them to try and excavate a burrow to reach that warm-blooded prey hidden deep in its depths. It is important never to do this unless you actually want a terrier to try and dig into a warren.

I kept Lakelands in the past, and they were exactly the same, learning early that rabbits are worked on top, and foxes are the things you go to ground on. Even the good little earth dog I have at the moment, a black bitch called Beetle, has never shown the slightest desire to dig on to a rabbit. She would have made a good ferreting dog had I been inclined to use her for that job, for she marks inhabited burrows a treat.

The terriers I keep now, and have kept for nearly 20 years, are a bitch line of mongrelly Russell types. I call them Russell 'types' because they are, for the most part, white bodied, though

I couldn't say exactly what breeds went into their make-up, and nor do I care. They wouldn't win shows and most are snipey-muzzled, but they do what I want and are easy to live with as well. They are certainly as good in cover as any I've seen, and they are biddable too and not quarrelsome with other dogs.

~ NOT A RUSSELL TYPE ~

I do have one terrier which is not of the Russell type. Beetle's temperament is typical of the dour, killing dogs from the north, and although she works well in the field with no hint of animosity towards the other terriers, I'd never allow her to run loose in the yard, for her fuse is measured in milli-seconds, not minutes. When Beetle's energy can be focused on work she is perfectly well-behaved and capable of working alongside other dogs with no problem at all, but that simmering need to crunch and kill never sleeps. It merely slumbers darkly, deep in the very core

Beetle with fox from a very wet drain.

of her being, waiting to burst into flames at the slightest of touches.

Interestingly enough, Beetle can work the beating line on a shoot all day long, putting up pheasants and the occasional rabbit as well as any spaniel, and she even retrieves to hand, though the game she presents to me might be a tad 'marked'! Slightly squashed would be a better description, though she's never yet broken the skin of a rabbit. She just has to crunch them a bit to make sure that they're dead, you understand, which doesn't matter to me for we don't sell our rabbits; they are destined only for home consumption, be that for us, the dogs or the ferrets.

Beetle was given to me by some lovely people up north, whom I've never even met. A leap of faith on my part as well as theirs, for not only was I a stranger to them, I also knew very little of the working credentials of the pup's ancestors. The tiny blob of black fur was ferried down to this end of the country by a third party at the age of six weeks. Both were acts of great generosity: first, the gift of the pup herself, and second, the subsequent means of her arrival, proving once again that, in an age where money so often shouts loudest, the working dog world is peopled with some genuine souls who are not motivated by greed. I learned very quickly that Beetle was a natural retriever, not a talent for which these hard black dogs are well-known. Not only will she retrieve a tennis ball endlessly, demanding encore after encore, long after my arm has got tired, but she retrieves rabbits as well, from anywhere and over any distance. From the depths of brambles so thick you'd need a digger to get into their midst, to ultra-long retrieves over the full length of a large field.

So possessive is Beetle that a pack-caught rabbit is quickly left to her jaws alone, and she never so much as utters a growl or a snarl. She doesn't need to. The other dogs just know that what Beetle grabs, Beetle keeps, and I've honestly never seen her aggress another dog in a dispute over a carcase of any sort. Lurchers and terriers alike, pack-caught rabbits are left to the little black bitch, and very quickly too, considering the verve of a pack on a kill. Once she has made sure that the rabbit is absolutely and completely dead, she brings it to my feet. This is indeed a handy talent to have when you're working deep brambles. Before

Beetle retrieving rabbit.

her arrival, I sometimes had to leave rabbits where they lay in some thorny jungle, inaccessible to me or the lurchers.

I have tried, and failed, to get my own line of terriers to retrieve rabbits, and whilst they will happily fetch balls and dummies, they refuse to countenance the bringing of a rabbit to hand if it has been caught in cover. Of course this might have something to do with the fact that there is seldom just one rabbit in the immediate area, and they're normally off hunting again the moment a bunny is dead. Beetle has what I call the Xtra factor, that extra aptitude for carrying things back to me. Like Elka the lurcher, Beetle is a dog apart from the rest. Like Elka, she neither plays nor mixes with the other dogs when not working, and like Elka, her mission in life is to kill and bring me that kill.

She is a very efficient killer, and although she's not had as much work to ground as she might have done in other hands, we've never yet dug to a live fox once engaged by Beetle. In fact, she even tries to retrieve her foxes, pushing and pulling the carcase (yes, it's always a carcase by this time) to the surface. The only time I have heard her bay was when a fox had wedged itself tight round a sharp corner in an old rabbit warren where it had been run to ground. From its inaccessible refuge it made life hard for the little black bitch for a while, though the baying didn't last long, and was soon replaced with that familiar grunting and bumping you associate with a terrier fast to its fox.

To be honest, Beetle is rubbish in cover compared to my Russelly types. It's not a lack of nose, or she'd be no good on the beating line, but she's learned not to bust a gut for bunnies in cover, especially when there are other dogs doing all the hard work. I don't really mind this attitude, because she is of course, at her best when facing old foxy deep in the dark, or anywhere for that matter. Read on, and yes, while the dog is the true star of this shred of a tale, yours truly deserves a mention, if only for behaving like a complete muppet. Oh yes, a fox hunt of any description still has the power to make me come over all childishly excited and eager, too eager.

~ THE DUNGHEAP FOX ~

We had gone to a friend's farm to avail ourselves of a large amount of beautifully rotted-down cow manure for use on our vegetable garden. Years and years of muck from the cattle barns had been dumped within the four walls of an old crewyard; a concrete-walled and roofless square, and whilst as a yard it may have long since ceased to serve its original purpose, as a container for liquid muck and soiled straw, it worked pretty well. The muck-heap reached almost halfway up the walls, which were house roof height, and all we had to do was park our van on the track which ran alongside the building, then shovel the oldest and best of the muck into bags, from where the sides of the heap had crumbled and spilled out over the top of one side. It was lovely stuff, rich and dark and full of red worms: broken down organic matter in the finest stage of decay; perfect for enriching the earth in our garden.

Rat runs wove in and out of every level of the heap, and we'd taken the three terriers along for the ride, not really expecting to find many rats in the bright daylight hours, but it was something to occupy the tykes for an hour or so whilst we worked on filling our fertilizer bags with muck.

"Watch out for that bit in the middle," I warned Andy, as I stood on the top of the heap, pointing down to a suspiciously damp patch of straw which lay in a depression right in the middle of the muck heap. "It looks a bit soft down there."

The terriers busied themselves by hunting along the walls, poking their noses into the holes, though not trying to dig. There can't have been much scent as Beetle soon tired of investigating the entrances. She pottered across the undulating and steaming straw to the opposite wall, where a great pile of rubble lay piled. Broken concrete blocks, rusted sheets of corrugated iron, bricks, and bits of timber: general farm-type debris all piled high to make a great hiding place for wildlife, and now Beetle was trying to find a way under the rubbish.

Before I could stop her she'd vanished, squeezing in through the tiniest of gaps between two lumps of concrete. Midge followed closely behind the little black bitch, and I clambered over the heap to investigate, my senses on full alert. Sometimes you get a feeling that something more interesting is about to happen, and I guess that this almost instinctive reaction comes from years and years of working with dogs.

We read our dogs' body language without consciously being aware of it, and from the corner of my eye, as I stood on the muck-heap, I'd clocked a change in Beetle's behaviour as she made her way to the rubble pile. I knew that she was scenting something which wasn't a rat. Seconds later a volley of muffled yaps filtered out from the pile of rubble, followed by Beetle's trade mark bumping and grunting. Young Nickel was running about on top of the rubble, all excited but not really knowing what was going on.

Then I smelled fox.

166

I called Andy and asked him to give me a hand in removing some rubble, hoping that the fox wouldn't be too deep under all that concrete and timber, for the whole pile teetered dangerously: concrete on timber, timber on bricks, layer upon layer piled higgledy-piggledy, and laced through with razor-sharp old rusted tin.

I circumnavigated the oozing depression in the middle of the muck-heap to fetch dog leads from the back of the van. I needed to get Nickel tied up and out of the way, and now Midge, who'd come out and was trying to dig in from another angle, obviously unable to get past Beetle. The last thing I wanted was for these terriers to damage themselves on those sharp shards and lumps.

Just as I turned to come back past the heap, leads in hand, Andy shouted: "I'm through", and (as if you haven't guessed by now!) muggins, in her enthusiasm and hurry to be 'in at the kill' decided to take the short cut straight across the top of the heap, completely forgetting that sinister puddle of ooze in the

Beetle in rubble.

middle. That soggy depression which I'd avoided so carefully only moments before might as well not have been there, such was the power of the fox to drive all else from my mind. And yes, with the reddest of faces and great embarrassment, I admit I ran full tilt into that swamp, right up to my hips in liquid manure.

I was stuck fast, sinking slowly deeper and deeper into the mire. Cold liquid filled my boots, and clutched my legs in an icy embrace, and I let out a pathetic squawk: "Help! I'm sinking!"

To be honest, for one brief moment I was actually scared, imagining my disappearance beneath the bubbling surface. My lifeless corpse would be food for the red worms, and later my bones would litter the fields, bleak testimony to a most horrible death. That moment of fear quickly passed when I realised that I had stopped sinking any deeper. And then I started to curse, having completely forgotten that our friend's father had dropped by to see how we were doing on the muck heap. I'm afraid that I shattered forever any illusions that gentleman may have entertained as to my feminine sensibilities, for the expletives that filled the air would have done a sailor proud, until Andy, who was laughing uproariously, yanked me from that stinking bog hole, damn near dislocating my arm in the process. In the end I had to swallow my wounded pride and join in the laughter whilst I removed and emptied my boots and wrung out my socks, which forever after remained an interesting shade of pale brown, no matter how many times I washed them.

The smell was nowhere near as bad as you'd imagine, because it was after all, good organic muck from herbivores, which in time rots down to produce an odour which, whilst not Chanel Number Five, is several degrees more acceptable than the odours which permeate from human sewage farms or chicken sheds.

Beetle had by now dispatched the fox with her normal efficiency, and luckily, she was less than a foot into the rubble, wedged between two lengths of timber which, fortunately for all of us, held the surrounding concrete quite safely in place. It only remained to dispose of the carcase and make safe the pile of rubble once more, before loading up the van and making our way home. I was soggy and stinking and mortally ashamed of my stupidity, but Andy beside me was attempting, and failing, to contain his mirth! Thank God he hadn't got his mobile with him or no doubt my plight would have been recorded for posterity, and honesty would have forced me to include the photo in this book.

~ THE RUSSELLY THINGS ~

These little white-bodied dogs have provided me and the lurchers with so much sport over the years that their exploits would fill a dozen books. The fact that I'm still only on the fourth generation of these handy workers, shows how useful and sensible they are. Old Sonic worked hard until she was about 12 years of age, both to ground and on top, and despite the fact that I kept retiring

The original Midge and pups.

Sonic, her daughter Silver, and her two pups Copper and Nickel.

her from earth work, she tottered along in her old age, defiantly intent on finding her favourite quarry to ground.

I fully admit that these dogs aren't a line as such, and I simply mated each bitch to a dog that I liked, regardless of his breeding. In fact, Sonic, Midge's daughter, was the result of a mating to a little farmyard terrier I'd met on my pest control rounds. Dog and bitch looked good side by side, and whilst hardly the most scientific reasoning behind such a mating, there was something about the dog that I liked, and he was working bred, even though his duties around the farm consisted merely of ratting and rabbiting.

I very reluctantly put Sonic in the ground in early spring, 2012; she was nearly 17 years of age, and her quality of life hadn't been much for the past year or so. She spent most of her time curled up asleep, and although she came instantly to life at the prospect of food, she was weak, totally deaf and beginning to look as though the end was fast approaching. As Andy shovelled the final resting place for the little white bitch, I remembered her very last fox, at the age of 15!

170

~ SONIC'S LAST FOX ~

We'd gone out for a walk in late winter, a fine sunny day it was, and one of the few times that Sonic decided she'd come out with the other dogs. I'd pretty much let her decide how to pass her later years and most days she simply stayed on the sofa when the other dogs ran to the door at the sound of jingling keys. This day, for some reason unknown, maybe it was the warming air, that indefinable aura which tells us that winter has finally loosened its grip on the land for another year, or maybe the old dog just happened to wake at the moment I'd picked up my keys, for the sound had jolted her fading senses into action.

We pottered slowly along the edge of a long field bright with young wheat shining green in the sunlight, and whilst the younger terriers busied themselves in the dyke bottom, harassing the rabbits beneath the brambles, Sonic trotted steadily behind me, her nose, as always, to the ground. Her sense of smell was the one thing she clung to during those last few years of life, for her eyes were no longer as sharp as they'd been in her youth.

I tried to keep half an eye on the bitch, for, deaf as she was, she soon became disorientated if she lost sight of the pack, but then of course I forgot all about her as a rabbit bolted back down the dyke, followed by screaming terriers and bouncing lurchers. Moments later I turned to look for the old girl, but she was nowhere to be seen! A curse left my lips, an automatic reaction of concern for a tired old dog, but she couldn't have gone far. Logically she was incapable of moving at more than a trot, and then all at once young granddaughter Nickel, still a pup, began staring intently into a hole on the bank.

And I heard baying from under my feet!

To my credit, the traitorous thought which flashed into my head was gone in a second, and I didn't truly believe that Sonic had gone on a rabbit. Why would she? She'd never once tried to get into a rabbit hole in her entire life, unless a fox happened to be in residence at the time; she wasn't so senile that the work ethics of a lifetime could have vanished, so I made the inevitable phone call, asking Andy to bring Midge, Sonic's daughter, collar and spade. Luckily I was only five minutes from our house, and even luckier, Andy was home for the evening.

He arrived soon after, and all the while Sonic had kept up her incessant baying literally beneath my feet. I'd restrained the pup, and put Beetle on a lead, tied up out of the way, and once Midge had entered all baying had ceased.

It took only a couple of spadefuls of earth before we broke through, and there was Sonic, not baying now, but tugging determinedly on a deep red brush which was clenched between her broken and lopsided teeth. The fox dispatched, we lifted both terrier and fox to discover that somehow, God only knows how, Midge had pushed over both fox and her dam to engage the pointy end of her quarry. With the tube being no more than a rabbit burrow, I still can't figure out how Midge managed this Houdini-like feat, but she did, and I was pleased that the old bitch hadn't had to face the teeth at her advanced age. She must have followed her nose when the fox flashed to ground, no doubt put up by the other dogs working the dyke. Strangely, the other terriers had already passed that entrance as they worked up the dyke bottom.

Sonic tottered home none the worse for wear, and I couldn't help but admire the old girl. I know that dogs have no conscious realisation in their heads that they might be too old or weak to work, but it showed that she'd lost none of the desire and nose for work, even if the rest of her body was crumbling with age.

~ THE SECOND MIDGE ~

I've always been superstitious when it comes to naming pups, never using a name by which I'd named a dog in the past. For some reason I broke my own rule when the second Midge was born and I named her after her grandmother, maybe because the pup reminded me of that original Midge which I'd met on the road as a pup, even though they weren't remotely similar in appearance. Inside, where it counts, their heads were almost identical.

Young Midge is tri-coloured, the result of a surreptitious mating between Sonic and a large black and tan terrier, whose dam I had also bred many years previously. He was no relation to the Russelly line, being instead from the Lakeland side of things, with the infusion of some little hunt terriers I'd worked

Above: Sonic and Favour ...

Below: Sonic's nose still worked well into old age

for a while. I say surreptitious, for the dog belonged to a good friend of mine, and we were out for a day's digging on the fens. I'd 'carelessly' thrown both terriers loose into the back of the van at the end of the day, knowing full well that Sonic was in season at the time! It was one of those spur of the moment decisions I've made more than once in my life, and one that I've never regretted in the slightest. Midge turned out to be everything her grand-dam had been, and more. She barks at rabbits to move them from dense brambles, and she's likely to find a fox anywhere, including in trees, where they lie up inside the hollow branches of willows.

Willow trees tend to die from the inside out in great age, and whilst the sap is still carried up through a layer of living wood encircling the dying core, the middle of the trunk and even the interiors of the largest branches are often hollow and rotten. These trees make good hide-outs for foxes, especially during the wet season when the low-lying earths are flooded.

The second Midge.

The terriers have bolted many foxes from these hollow branches over the years, some leaping earthwards towards a waiting lurcher which dances, jaws snapping in anticipation beneath the long, horizontal boughs. Others do not or cannot bolt, encased in a stop-end of living wood which becomes a death-trap once a terrier scents the whereabouts of its quarry.

~ THE FOX IN THE TREE ~

The lurchers and terriers are following a line along the side of a shallow dyke which is flanked by willow trees. We are on a flood plain which is permanent pasture, prone to flooding whenever the rain fall is sufficient to swell the river in autumn, and sometimes in spring. Scent is always good here, for the water table is high all year round thanks to the rivers and lakes which surround us. Even in summer, the evening mist often spreads a blanket of moisture upon the grass, sprinkling great drops of dew on to spider webs, leaving a glistening, shimmering patchwork of silvery lace as far as the eye can see.

I watch the dogs working the line, and as usual, they are unhurried in their work. We can cover this ground every day for a week, sometimes a month, without seeing a fox, though the fields are criss-crossed with their runs and their scent. The dogs work quietly in the knowledge that their chances of actually finding a fox here by day are remote, unless they've been flooded out of the nature reserve. Just two fields away lies the nature reserve, out of bounds to the dogs, a dense 50-acre block of willows and reeds surrounding a lake, and the place is bursting at the seams with muntjac and foxes alike.

I used to come over all irritated and annoyed at the thought of so much game, so tantalisingly near, but so forbidden. Nowadays I'm rather pleased that this place exists, for without a 'safe house' I've no doubt that we'd have made some serious inroads into the local populations of both animals. They do, after all, need somewhere safe to breed.

Midge and Starlight are working together, noses glued to the ground, and now they're showing a little more interest in the scent. Midge is moving faster, as though she is picking up on the real possibility of a fox nearby. Then Starlight overtakes her,

175

galloping fast, looking up at the trees as she runs. There are three huge willows in a line, their towering branches spread wide as well as high, and all three are old with hollow trunks.

The dogs ignore the first two trees, and head straight for the third, and Starlight pushes her head into the crack of the split bole. Midge pushes under the lurcher's belly, and waits patiently until the sinewy, though too large body of the lurcher withdraws her head; there's no histrionics or barking or unnecessary excitement from the terrier, for she knows her turn will come, knows full well that the lurcher can't get into the tree herself.

Starlight struggles to pull her head out of the tree, almost panics, then lies down to get the angle right, twists her neck sideways and shoots backwards in a heap, shaking her head hard to ease the pain of her stinging ears. She would have scraped them hard against the bark as she struggled to extricate herself. Midge instantly forces her body into the gap, squeezing against the unyielding wood, and she vanishes from sight. The other lurchers mill about impatiently, but Starlight stands still with her nose to the crevice, breathing long breaths of her favourite scent.

Then there's banging and bumping from inside the tree. No barking or growling, just banging and I can feel the vibrations through my hands as I place them against the dry and corrugated bark of the old willow. I wait. Minutes pass, and I can only imagine at what is happening within the depths of the branch. I try and climb up a little, finding finger and toe holds, clinging on like a monkey, and as I gain a little height I can peer into the top of the hollow tube of the trunk.

The main trunk of this ancient willow is open to the sky, completely hollowed out, and partially full of red, rotting wood which has fallen down from the inner sides of the trunk. From a circular wall of still-living tree, the branches extend outwards, though they too are hollow, and there are three of them, forking out from the central cylinder of wood. I have no idea in which branch Midge is battling the fox as the sound is reverberating through the whole tree. I slip back to earth and sit with my back to the tree, feeling the faint tremors pulsing through the battered old giant, and although I'm not worried for Midge, the thought does cross my mind that if she gets stuck, I'll have to contact the

Above: A line of ancient hollow willows.

Below: Starlight tried to get into the tree.

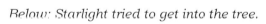

Three generations of terriers have been working these trees. Top: Old Midge and daughter Sonic. Bottom: Sonic's daughter Silver.

farmer who is the only one with a key to the field gate, and ask for help with a chainsaw!

I banish these thoughts from my mind for that is a worst-case scenario and we're not yet at that stage. I continue to wait, but now there is no more bumping, and I climb up the trunk once more and try to peer into the empty depths. And there is Midge's rear end, not moving, clearly visible at the entrance of one of the hollow branches. She's almost at ground level, and her body must be angled upwards into a wide crack up the inner surface of the hollow trunk; it no doubt leads into a branch. But the terrier is temporarily stuck, blocked by the dried lumps of wood which have fallen into the main trunk space, no doubt dislodged during the battle. She moves a little, and I realise she is pulling on something which I cannot see, but she's not shaking it very hard at all. She can't, for there's little or no room for her to move.

I lie down full length on the ground beneath the tree, and stretch my arm as far as I can into the hole, feeling chunks of rotting wood and bits of branches. I start to pull them out, one by one, having to break them up and twist them about in order to negotiate the curvature of the wood-bound entrance hole. You only realise how rigid wood is when you're trying to move wood within wood, and had the broken-off pieces not been rotten, I'd have never been able to manage this at all. Starlight is breathing down the back of my neck, standing over me impatiently, but she's not fired up and in kill mode; she knows that the fox must be dead, and her excitement level has subsided to a level of merely keen interest.

"Midge," I say to the terrier, and I can just see her tail as it wags in response to my voice. "Fetch it Midge." Although she has never retrieved anything other than a tennis ball in her life, reluctance to give up her prey makes her hang on to it tight as she reverses into the space I've cleared behind her.

She doesn't 'fetch it' of course, but she is able to pull her prize further into the open space, before turning to squeeze back out through the crack in the trunk, and now I can reach in to grab the carcase by one foot, and haul it out in the open. Starlight vents a little frustration on the fox but poor old Midge is standing to one side looking somewhat vague and disorientated.

Then I realise that her head is swollen and battered; her ears are hot and tender, sticking out at right angles and although there's hardly a bite on her muzzle, she must have, during the heat of the battle, repeatedly pummelled her head against the hard wooden walls of the branch; she sways on her feet a little, and having stashed the carcase in a nearby ditch, pushing it into the oozing mud out of sight, I pick Midge up and carry her back to the van. After a couple of hundred metres the terrier is fidgeting in my arms, and I put her back down on the ground, whereupon she dives straight into a bramble and flushes a rabbit. How can anyone not admire and respect the toughness and drive of a terrier?

Midge has seldom been to ground officially, as I don't dig much these days, but she has the same determination as her grandmother when it comes to finding foxes, and she's more intelligent and tougher than her dam, Sonic. Sonic has always been good, but the two Midges, two generations apart, have always been that bit 'more' in every way.

When you are breeding for a specific trait, such as nose in a line of bushing dogs, pot-luck plays a part, especially in a line which isn't a line as such. I know that I should have done some serious in-breeding to fix those traits I like so much, but I'm a bit of a pot-luck individual myself, trusting to instinct and gut feel rather than scientific reasoning when it comes to breeding dogs. Most times I've been happy with what I've done, though sometimes when heart rules head, the outcome isn't quite what you'd expect. Life would be boring if the results were set in stone before you choose a course of action.

I wish I had more room in this book to recount the terriers' exploits. Times change, I no longer dig, but I can never imagine a life without them. They've provided the lurchers with more sport than you'd believe possible over the years, and even today, in a world full of too many laws and restrictions, I seldom set out for a walk without a terrier by my side. Even if I'm forced to keep it leashed for more of the time than I did in the old days, there's usually a place where the small dog can give us some fun by bolting something from a bramble, be it only a rabbit or two. Life's seldom boring when you have a handy terrier: I owe them so much.

180

Sonic (on left) and daughter Silver (by Marx) waiting in the bottom of the dyke at a dig.

~ Sparrow ~
~ and the dunking munty ~

I can honestly say that since the ban came in I've never actually gone out with the intention of finding a muntjac. However, when they insist on encroaching on previously 'munty-free' land, things can become a little fraught to say the least. To be honest they are becoming a bloody nuisance, throwing daily dog exercise into something approaching a reconnaissance mission into enemy territory.

Every time I pass by a brambly patch or a reed bed my senses are on high alert. Trouble is, so are those of the dogs! Muntjac can lie up as tight as a bug in a rose bud, or they can lose their nerve and leap out unexpectedly, right into your path. Chaos would be a good word to describe the ensuing scramble to arms when this happens.

The general public is usually quite unaware of their presence, as muntjac do sit tight in their bramble barracks if they think that their presence has gone unnoticed, and I've actually been standing within two metres of a muntjac lying still in the tiniest clump of reeds, and it only leapt up when I stared straight at its hiding place, though I was unaware that I'd been looking at anything other than a clump of grasses.

The main problem with exercising lurchers on public land where dog walkers wander from dawn until dusk is that the muntjac actually become very accustomed to being in close proximity to dogs on a regular basis. My problem is that whilst the average pet dog probably won't give chase in more than a very half-hearted manner, quickly losing the target in cover, my

Opposite: Sparrow.

dogs know all too well just how tasty a meal is hidden inside the little brown barrel of fur, and of course they're fast enough to bring that meal to the table.

Here's an account of one such incident which occurred whilst we were out on a nice peaceful walk. I'd taken my dogs to one of our usual haunts, a well-used footpath around the old gravel pits. The path is a long wide track between scraggly hedges of hawthorn and elder and the ever-present brambles; it's a good place where the dogs can burn off a bit of energy and it keeps them on their toes hunting the resident rabbits. Very occasionally they make a catch, but it's a bit like trying to pin down a mouse through all that thick cover. The rabbits seldom bolt into the open and are more likely to be luck-caught between the terriers inside the brambles rather than making a flash for safety in front of the lurchers.

I thought I was safe in allowing the Airedale to work the reed beds just to the left of the track and hedge as the only things she was likely to disturb were a few coots and moorhens. Until this day!

I'd timed my walk to coincide with as few dog walkers as possible, round about four o'clock in the afternoon, midway between the lunchtime crowd and the after-work walkers. I'm a loner by nature, and hate having to meet other people when I'm out with the dogs. Not only do I loathe having to make conversation with someone I don't know, but mid-afternoon is also one of the 'safest' times when it comes to avoiding accidental hunts on illegal quarry, most of the time.

I've been exercising my dogs in this area for nearly 25 years now, and in the early days it was unusual to meet anyone else at all. The gravel pits were still in operation, and nobody had created the signposted 'walks'. Our village was still almost a village, as opposed to a sprawling eruption of steadily-expanding housing estates, and I'd happily walk back to my van carrying a couple of rabbits in full view. No need to hide them from the shocked gaze of 21st century supermarket-fed people to whom meat comes in a plastic wrapped tray. I now put rabbits in my game bag which is disguised as a dog lead and 'treat' bag.

Nowadays I watch my dogs like hawks from the moment they step out of the van. I need to know what scent they are catching from the air, and I scan my horizons as far as I can, the better to be prepared for unwanted things, both people and wildlife.

The wildlife is also more adept at keeping discreetly away from the main thoroughfares during daylight, and these days I would never expect anything larger than a squirrel or a rabbit to cross my path whilst it is still light.

I allow Dill, the Airedale, to work the reed bed. She really needs to work, following that nose, finding scent and pushing through cover. As long as she's silent I know that she's only on small stuff or feather. I had four lurchers with me, old Starlight, her daughter Hunni the blond bimbo, her grumpy auntie Favour, and Sparrow, her ice-eyed merle niece.

'Sparrow stands at around 22 inches and is the result of a merle Collie Greyhound put back to a bitch from the rough-coated line I've maintained for over 20 years. She looks a bit like a hairy mongrel Collie with slightly longer legs, but her scruffy appearance hides a tight, streamlined body and behind those startling eyes of ice blue lurks the calculating brain of an efficient predator.

On the whole, the line throws decent mooching lurchers, capable of turning their paws to most things, though they don't have the out-and-out stamina and the gears to make top-notch hare dogs. They are pretty handy through cover, and while they might not make the catch every time when running through trees and thick vegetation, I'd sooner they come home in one piece, able to run the next day, than be possessed of that kamikaze brain which gets dogs killed in such country.

They say only the good die young, but there's good and clever, and there's good and not so clever. It's getting that balance right in a dog; getting a lurcher somewhere between the ones with too much brain and not enough drive, and the ones which don't have enough brain but have tons of drive. Getting this balance right has been a long and, at times, devastating journey. I like a dog with just enough common sense to handle itself on dangerous ground, though still retaining the drive which is necessary for the effort needed to make a kill. Let's get back to that 'incident'.

The lurchers are pottering about on the track before me, and we're barely five minutes into our walk. Dill, the Airedale, has lifted her head and gone straight to the reeds. I'm used to this behaviour. Dill always has to check out the hidden muntjac 'motorways' which lead through the reed beds, the paths they habitually use during their nocturnal wanderings. She'll follow a scent from the previous night for a short distance, with a degree of interest, but no real intent, for she knows that the line is cold. Today things will change, and even as I hear the sound of a big body crashing through the reeds I'm still too preoccupied with some inner thoughts to take note, and I realise too late that the Airedale is not on a cold trail at all.

A garbled howl breaks the silence. The yodelling cry is a cross between the bay of a fox hound and a giant terrier bark. It goes something like this: Row-wup! Row-wup! Row-wup! The song is short. She only bays when she puts something up; once it is moving and is out of her sight she falls silent again and concentrates on following the line. Dill only gives tongue on larger game, and her summons is a frustrated cry for help from the swift hounds.

Sparrow cooling down after a hard run.

Almost immediately, a muntjac breaks across the track, right between the lurchers, so close to Sparrow that it barely side-steps her instinctive strike, leaving the dogs spinning in its wake. The lurchers pour through the fence to my right, flying after the deer and into the next reed bed. I hear crashing and breaking of stems and old branches, then silence. Dill lumbers on to the track, doggedly following the ground scent, and she almost runs into me, intent on the delicious smell left by those tiny sharp hooves. I grab her quickly because deer and dogs have vanished in the direction of the fishing lakes, a privately-run syndicate where the carp men sit in their bivvies all the year round, and I really don't want that Airedale nose disturbing their reveries or advertising our presence.

One by one the lurchers come back to the path, first Hunni, then Favour and a moment later Starlight. But of Sparrow there's no sign at all. I wouldn't expect any dog to stay tight on the tail of a munty through cover like this, but Sparrow had been the closest behind the deer as it vanished. I put leads on the lurchers and wait for Sparrow, but she doesn't return and I begin to feel that familiar little niggle of worry and fear.

Is she injured? Or dead? Lying with neck broken against some tree? Been there, done it, or rather, seen it happen. 'Not again', I pray.

In this place it's all fallen branches, thick brambles and weeds. Banks of old sand, steep-sided and shifting, and ancient fences of barbed wire sagging from broken posts, derelict woodland where nature has pummelled and pushed her way into thick, luscious life on the margins of man's quest for gravel. Through it all are the reed beds which grow in great swathes, thick and tall, around the sides of every lake and pool. It's a dangerous place for a running dog at the best of times, but my lurchers have grown up learning the pitfalls and dangers from their early puppyhood, and in more than 25 years I've only had one dog come to grief here, and that was poor Rhino, victim of man-made rubbish in the form of that dumped bath tub.

Still I worry about little Sparrow, she's never been gone so long before. They either kill or lose their quarry quickly on this land, and I've heard no tell-tale screech to give me the news that the dog has caught its prey. A couple of minutes pass, then I hear a strange noise, not quite the ear-splitting scream of a stricken muntjac, but neither is it the howling of an injured dog. (That's another sound which strikes to the heart when your dog is out of sight, and one I dread hearing.) I listen again, the sound is faint, and it seems to be coming from somewhere along the banks of the lake to my right, a larger expanse of water several hundred yards from the first. The other dogs haven't heard the noise yet, for the breeze blows the noise high over their heads. Then there's silence again. I am puzzled. Once more comes the strangled screech, and this time I know it's a muntjac, but just what is going on?

Now the other dogs can hear the noise too, and they're straining in that direction. I begin to walk; no sense in running with four dogs on leads as I'd end up in a heap on the ground! Through the fence, over a bank, along a tiny footpath through brambles which snag and rip at my jeans, and every now and again I can hear that strangely muffled noise.

I can hear the sound for a moment, then it ceases for a little while before starting up again, and so it goes on. Why hasn't Sparrow killed it by now? What is stopping her normally efficient predator jaws from throttling the beast? I know she's only small, but she has the power and skill to finish her quarry with no problem at all.

I'm heading now to the main footpath round the big lake, and the squawking is getting louder. I begin to get that familiar twist in my stomach, that fear of discovery, because now I'm on the footpath, the main dog-walker route and the noise is very near. I quicken my pace, helped just a bit by the dogs as they try and tow me along. I am forced to release Dill because she is straining, head down, like a Bulldog towing a car. Not the quick surge of the sighthound, but the urgent and repeated, powerful lunges that can get a dead weight started from a standstill. I am sure that she'll help Sparrow finish the job by the time I get there, but even after she's vanished into a stand of tall trees next to the path, the damned noise goes on!

Then I'm running down the wide gravel path, doing a sterling impression of a charioteer minus his chariot, towed along by the galloping dogs, and we launch ourselves down a sloping bank into the trees, and come across Dill and Sparrow ... in three feet of water, the muntjac between them, and suddenly I understand

188

the problem. I manage to grab one of its hind feet and pull it from the water to deliver the coup de grace, and even as I do so the beast turns its head to bite my arm. Luckily it is held from its intent by the Airedale.

Sparrow looks like a drowned rat; exhausted. She's coughing up copious amounts of water and a small gash leaks watery pink blood all down the soggy white fur of her throat. Dill is soaked too, and no wonder. I won't realise until much later that the muntjac has laid the side of her neck open in a deep wound that goes into the muscle. The gash is, for the moment, hidden beneath the thick wet, black fur of her neck, and as usual she gives no indication at all that she is injured. Her pain threshold is so high that I imagine she'd be dead before she admitted defeat in anything she undertook.

Airedales were used extensively as messenger dogs during the First World War, their extreme determination and resilience making them ideal for such work in horrendous conditions. There are stories of Airedales, shot and wounded by shrapnel and bullets, staggering on to complete their missions before collapsing and dying once they'd delivered their packages to the troops. I can well believe these stories, because nothing, but nothing, deflects Dill once she's fixed on a mission to track her game to its source.

I can only guess at the exact turn of events. First, I'm incredibly impressed at how Sparrow managed to keep on the tail of her prey through all that rubbish and undergrowth. Deer and dog must have gone at least 500 yards through the sort of cover which normally leaves the lurchers floundering unsighted, but she'd stuck like a burr to her quarry.

However, she'd come unstuck when the muntjac leapt into a wide deep ditch full of water. She must have leapt into the ditch on top of her prey, and struggling to find her normal throat-hold, had found herself submerged. I could now make sense of those intermittent cries. Each time the dog found the throat of her prey, both animals would have ended up under the surface of that brown, brackish water, and after a few seconds Sparrow must have released her grip to come up for air. Likewise the muntjac, struggling to fight off the dog, until she managed to seize its neck once more, thereby forcing it under the water all over again.

189

This obviously happened several times as I was making my way to the pair, and even once Dill was on hand, that terrier brain hadn't thought to try and pull the deer on to dry land. Dill might be smart, but she's still a terrier when all's said and done, and she wouldn't have reasoned that one out, just dived in for the kill! This muntjac was a large, mature male, well-endowed with fearsome fangs and slanting sharp-tipped horns, and I was very lucky that it had not inflicted more damage on the dogs.

Lucky us in more ways than one! Once again, the Gods of the hunt had smiled upon us, for no passer-by came wandering along the path. No doubt the squawks, had anyone actually heard the noise, would have been attributed to the strangely prehistoric cries of herons as they rose, disturbed from their fishing positions at the edges of the lake.

I concealed the carcase beneath a thick layer of dead leaves near the base of a tree. I'd return to claim it later, once it was dark, minus my dogs of course, though I usually take a leashed terrier with me just in case I've forgotten the exact whereabouts of my prize in the shadowy woods.

Not only have I been extremely lucky over the years in that our occasional accidents have gone unnoticed by the general public, but I've seldom had dogs badly damaged either. The worst incident occurred many, many years ago when I first lived in this area. I had a very useful little lurcher, a dainty creature of around 24 inches, who was normally adept at handling herself on a variety of quarry, but she came unstuck when a muntjac laid her shoulder open, right down the length of the shoulder blade, actually exposing the bone in the process.

This had been no home staple-it-yourself affair, for the underlying muscle had been slit open as deeply as if a razor-sharp butcher's knife had been wielded. My vets, a very understanding couple whose hunting hearts were almost as keen as mine, had anaesthetised the dog and sewn her back up with both internal and external stitches within the space of an hour. I even paid half the resulting bill with some generous cuts from the beast that had caused all the trouble: the saddle and a hind leg, all beautifully butchered and prepared for the oven. Those were the days!